get your

out of college

For Patty and Kathy
who sought education
and were given schooling

get your

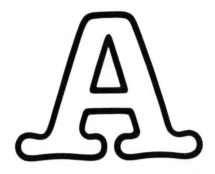

out of college

mastering the hidden rules of the game

Clark McKowen

Crisp Publications, Inc.
Los Altos, California

10 9 8 7 6 5

ISBN 0-931961-37-8
Library of Congress Catalog Number 78-71466
Printed in the United States of America

CONTENTS

Contents

Contents

A PROMISE

This book will get you through school with top grades. You won't be frustrated and you won't waste any time. You will gain some leisure hours, and you will feel so good you may choose to use them to educate yourself—since no one else can do it for you. But that is your own business. No doubt you have had plenty of advice on that already.

School *is* a wonderful place for education. Somebody ought to try it sometime. For most people, school builds in so many distractions that it seems the chance to think things through will never come. And most find their grades depressingly consistent. How frustrating to know you are a B student . . . forever. Does anyone really like being less than an A? Your college knows when you enter, or can find out, what your grade-point average will likely be throughout your stay.[1] From one point of view, school provides an atmosphere in which failure is the rule and success is rare.

But school *is* a wonderful place for an education. Books, buildings, optimum age, intelligent associates, enthusiasm— everything going for it and yet . . . what a drag!

The problem is that school and what you and I know is *education* are not the same thing. (They do sometimes coincide.) Education, as you well know, throbs in the veins, sets the nerves tingling, peels the eyeball, sears the intellect, and makes the hair stand up on your neck. It is thrilling, frightening, and alive. It can happen anywhere. But school too often is plodding through assignments and following rules. It is proper behavior, multiple-choice tests, 500-word themes, teacher monologs, grade-point averages, padded and poorly written texts, competition. In other words, it is a game you are expected to play, often without knowing the actual rules and goals.

While you may innocently assume the goal is mastery of your subject, you are being sorted, ranked, graded, and labeled.[2] By the time you are out of school, your A, B, C, D, or F label will be permanent. Not only does the registrar record your label, but your friends, parents, grad school, and

---

[1] See Wayne Jennings and Joe Nathan, "Startling /Disturbing Research on School Program Effectiveness," *Phi Delta Kappan*, March, 1977.
[2] See Leo Ruth, "Standardized Testing: How to Read the Results," SLATE Steering Committee Newsletter, NCTE/SLATE, Urbana, Illinois.

employers will think of you that way, too. You may even come
to accept it yourself. "Oh, I was always a C student."

    This arrangement is considered reasonable and normal by
the rule-makers and even by most of the players. The school
game calls for the failure of 95 per cent of the players. Those
testing in the top five per cent are considered to have succeeded. The rest to some degree have not. In some instances
schools themselves may actually *cause* poor student performance.[3] And, of course, the rank you fall in is totally artificial.
It is no predictor of how well you will do in real life. There is
no necessity for the game to be set up this way. It is not a law
of life.

    Not only do many schools build in excessive failure, they
do not even expect that much will be learned or retained, even
by A students. Most teachers know that nine-tenths of what is
taught will not be retained beyond the final exam. You can ver-
ify this fact by examining the residue in your own mind.
Schools accept these depressing results as part of the game.
Most teachers are happy if they can occasionally reach three or
four students in a class.

    It may come as a surprise, then, that it is quite possible for
95 per cent of an average group of college students to achieve
success. Numerous studies confirm this. Benjamin Bloom and
his colleagues at the University of Chicago, for example, designed a game in which 95 per cent (the top five per cent and
the next 90 per cent) achieved the goals specified.[4] Bloom did it
not by watering down the expectations but by changing the
learning atmosphere. These experiments expect long-term retention not of a mere one-tenth of what is learned but eight-
tenths or better.

**Ninety-five per cent master and retain eight-tenths of
what is taught.**

---

[3]K. Patricia Cross, *Beyond the Open Door* Jossey-Bass, 1971.
[4]"Learning for Mastery," UCLA-CSEJP, Evaluation Comment, 1, no. 2, 1968.

Imagine a game in which almost all students of French can count on mastering it, students of auto mechanics can become masters of their craft, students of geometry can fully expect to achieve mastery. When you think of it, that is not at all unreasonable. As John Carroll points out, recent evidence shows that it is not even necessary to have talent in a field to master it.[5] You don't even have to like it.[6] If you are mentally and physically okay—not great, just okay—you can master anything you feel like trying: painting, music, gymnastics, whatever.

Why haven't schools rushed to adopt these practices? It may be that mastery and achievement are simply not the purposes of schooling. For many, sorting and ranking are. "How could we tell a B student from a D? What would business, industry, or grad schools do if we sent out nothing but A students?" And you may be thinking that, too. If you are so accustomed to ranking that you wouldn't want to be part of a school in which 95 per cent get top grades, don't worry. These massive institutions are not about to change over. Meanwhile, you can easily get those A grades that only five per cent are allowed to have. All you have to do is discover the actual goals and learn how to play the real game. It will be far easier than you might imagine.

This book will show you the hidden rules of the game and show you how to play to win. Were you ever taught how to remember, how to take a test, how to cut through the padding in a text, how to keep the knots out of your stomach? If you are one who already knows how the game works, this book may show you how to play it better.

What you need to learn is how to learn.

School *is* a wonderful place to get an education. What follows may gain you the time and peace of mind to start.

---

[5]John B. Carroll, "A Model of School Learning," *Teachers College Record*, 64, 1963.
[6]John B. Carroll, "Problems of Measurement Related to the Concept of Learning for Mastery," *Educational Horizons*, 48, no. 3, 1970.

HOW TO USE THIS BOOK

> **To get the main points of this page, read the bold print.**

This book is intended to increase your alternatives. These extra choices will give you an edge in a game with hidden rules and goals. Take what you want. Don't turn it into a textbook. You have enough drudgery to contend with already. Enjoy yourself. As you go along, you will realize how capable you already are and how to make your strength pay off.

Step One

The dumbest thing you could do and something grade getters never do is just to start in reading. So don't do that. **Stop a minute.** Ask

What do I need from this book right now?

For all you know, it might not even be what you want or you may need just a fact or two for now. So **stop**.

Leaf through and see what sort of book this is. Find out if it will give you the kind of information you want.

The table of contents will give you the main topics, but it can't give you the feel of the material, so,

browse.

It will save you time in the long run.

Then, if you can use them,

Return here for some more tips on how to get the most from this book with the least wasted time.

To sum up this first step, browse to find out if this book is for you and if you can use it right now. (You must have had some reason for picking it up.) Maybe you will find what you need for the moment. In that case you might want to put the book back on your shelf until you need it again. If you want to understand the whole thing, go on to the suggestions given in Step Two.

But don't spend one minute more than you really need.

You have enough busywork as it is.

Step Two

If you followed our directions this far, you already have seen how the book is organized. There are two main ways to use it.

IMMEDIATE INFORMATION

For specific, immediate needs, find your topic in the table of contents. If you don't see it, try the index. Turn to the section or page indicated. Ideas and tips are in **boldface** or preceded by a ; sometimes both.

Go to the heading you want and read the bold print.

If necessary, read surrounding information to fill in gaps in your understanding.

MASTERY AND ABSORPTION

Read each chapter as thoroughly as your purpose requires. That does not mean that you have to read every word in it, only what you need. But for thorough understanding, first grasp the pattern and context in which your needed information is located. Read the synopsis and examine the outline at the beginning of each chapter. Then browse through, getting an impression of the chapter in general. Read the summary.

Next, each chapter starts with a few paragraphs giving the point of view from which the material can best be understood. Read that.

From this point on, whatever your purpose is, let it guide your reading. Master the entire chapter, or skip to just the part you want.

Sooner or later, when you are ready, read through the chapter from beginning to end at a fairly rapid rate. That will round out your grasp of main ideas and will help you to see their relationship to each other. This overview will strengthen your memory traces and will make it easier for you to absorb the ideas permanently.

Finally, if you want thorough understanding, apply the last two steps of the BFAR study-reading method which appears in Chapter Three, page 103.

1

Memorizing

IN THIS CHAPTER

SYNOPSIS

The best way to get good grades is to train your memory. This chapter begins with three general rules (pay attention, paraphrase, connect) and gives an example of how to commit them to memory. Then follow thirteen specific techniques, arranged from simple to more complex but more efficient. These, you can put to immediate use. Good memory comes from filing things well in the first place.

Next is a method for compressing the thirteen techniques into five meaningful groups. A recall 'quiz' helps reinforce your memory of the techniques. Some additional reinforcing aids are suggested.

Then come eleven retrieval strategies with strong emphasis on persistence and on trying alternatives. A trouble-shooting section shows how to overcome three basic interferences: panic, wrong filing strategies, and wrong recall tactics.

The summary connects memory training with ordinary thinking and problem solving, pointing out that the two processes are essentially the same.

MEMORY, THE MOST NEEDED SKILL

What is the main requirement in playing the school game? Intelligence? Talent? Hard work? Honesty? None of these is as important, if needed at all, as being able to remember things. Review your own schooling (you will have to use memory skill to do it) and you will find just about every course you have taken required retrieval of information as a main task, quite often the only one, needed in passing the course. Schools profess to value thinking but rarely do they teach or test for it. They test for facts, and recall of facts calls for memory strategies.

But course objectives and teachers' plans almost never provide for memory training. This most needed skill is ignored. It is as though memory training would make it too easy for students to win. The deck is stacked.

Meanwhile, dutiful students spend most of their time trying to remember and usually doing a rotten job of it. Grade getters stumble on a few techniques, and that usually gets them through. But most students don't.

Ironically, *the least effective memory method is* the one most commonly used: *passive repetition*, going over and over a list of unconnected facts. If you learn nothing else from this chapter, don't do that any more. It doesn't work. It is monotonous, wasteful, and useless. The results are disappointing and depressing. Just about anything else you try will probably work better.

What is effective? A little further on are specific tips ready for immediate use, but first here are three things you must do to get the stuff stored in your memory banks where you can find it later on. This is not a pep talk. It has been proven experimentally over and over. You have to use these three rules or you will forget. It is your time and your game. This is your first chance to change the odds.

GENERAL RULES FOR MEMORIZING

Pay attention. Your mind must be active. If it isn't, stop. You are wasting your time. Later in this chapter we will show you a method you can use to force yourself to pay attention.

Put it in your own words. "What exactly am I trying to remember? What is it like that I already know?" If you can say it another way, you have gone far toward memorizing it. If it makes sense to you, it is more likely to stick.

Connect. Fit whatever you can together into some framework or pattern. Then keep expanding the picture. Tie all that in with things you already know. That is, **organize**. Make room for your new pattern in some other pattern already inside you

If you can't remember material you are working on, chances are you have left out one or more of the three requirements. So it is a good idea to memorize them. Let's work on that.

A Model

Here is a sample of a procedure for remembering. Naturally, it doesn't take up nearly as much space or time to think through the process as it does to transcribe it here.

Let's see: What are the three requirements? **Attending, rephrasing,** and **connecting**. [Notice, I've rephrased the rules slightly. That will assist my memory a bit. That's Rule 2.] **Attending, rephrasing,** and **connecting.** *I want to bunch them together. One good word is better than three. For me, the word* **connect** *really involves all three, so that will work.* [You should find some word of your own—like **arc**. The search will help fix the idea in mind. That's Rule 1.]

   Connect *works for me because to connect I have to attend* **actively** *to the task* [Rule 1], *and, further, I automatically have to select a word I think will do the job* [Rule 2]. *So I have all three.* [Notice I am also **compressing** the task into the briefest form possible—easier to haul around in my mental filing system. And **connect** has enough *connections* to make it fairly easy to retrieve.] **Connect.**

   That's one connection. I think I will search around for some more. The more **links** [different word for *connect*, Rule 1] *the more chance I have of finding the three rules when I scan my memory bank later on. I notice that these three elements are also necessary for* **reading, taking tests, listening, note taking,** *and* **thinking** *in general. In other words they are basic to most thinking activities, most of the things one is required to do in school. These are* **problem-solving** *skills.* [And, as you read this book, you will see that attending to meaning (Rule 1), putting the task into your own words (Rule 2), and combining the new material with your own inner patterns (Rule 3), will be reinforced in each chapter. They will be new settings and new topics, but your behavior will be essentially the same. You have one simple principle to remember instead of dozens and dozens.]

   Now I have transformed the General Rules for Memorizing *into a* **web** *of meaning I myself created and understand. The word* **web** *should call up the ideas of* **connecting, rephrasing,** *and* **paying attention.**

Notice one more thing about my process in remembering these rules: I *do* repeat the elements I want to remember. However, I don't just chant the data over and over. Instead, information is repeated to keep it looping in front of me while I am processing it and fixing it in my filing system. Mere repetition alone has no chance at all of sticking, but **meaningful practice at the right time does help.** It acts as a holding pattern while I am finding links to retain it permanently. But, remember, repetition is always a short-term measure.

> **Keep in mind that memory is interconnections, and it is a system. The key is organization, connecting a new item to other items in the structure. All memory devices are based on this concept.**

MEMORY: MNEMONICS

There are lots of possible memory devices. If you have some of your own that are better, by all means use them. But do use some device. If you get something into your memory somehow but can't find it again, it is as if it is not there at all. Memory is another way of saying **system.** Tagging and cross-referencing for easy recovery make all the difference. A library full of books without a filing system is hopeless; everything depends on it. The methods of memory experts reveal that **memory is not so much a talent as it is a way of organizing data so they can be found quickly.** Even memory experts will forget all sorts of things, like people's names, if they neglect to file them properly. They, too, use name tags at their conferences. Grade getters don't have better memories, nor do geniuses—at least not enough to matter. But those who get the grades do have more effective filing systems. If you put a bit of information in there somewhere and can't find it when you want it, obviously you need a better method. If you have a bin for each new bit of data, you will become so top heavy and your system so messy, you won't be able to retrieve anything. You may be familiar with the problem.

However, if you understand what you have just read, you already have all the memory skills you could possibly need to get good grades. You just need to become conscious of the good techniques you already use.

Become conscious of the effective techniques you already use.

Start to list all the things you remember perfectly and you will soon fill a book and probably several: tying your shoes, where the sun comes up, where it goes. Realizing you remember so much should be heartening. There is nothing wrong with your memory. What you need are some deliberate filing and organizing techniques and some ways to find what you filed. And the more thoroughly you process the data the easier they will be to recall. Following are some memory strategies and after that some suggestions for recall and retrieval.

Thirteen Memory Strategies

These strategies will save you considerable time, and, as you will see, they work. Several experiments have demonstrated the value of learning memory techniques. In one such experiment, two groups were given the same material to learn and the same amount of time. The first group was simply told to learn the material and given no suggestions. In the other group the experimenter took up most of the time teaching memory techniques. The group had only a small part of the time left to learn the material. Their recall, however, was eight times better than that of the first group.

1. Rhyme

Example

i before e except after c
or when sounded as a
as in **neighbor** and **weigh.**

Remember that from grade school? The **rhyme** technique is still a powerful memory device. And a nonsense verse often sticks better than a sensible one. Sometimes we wish we *could* get rid of a TV jingle or a catchy lyric. That is one reason poets use rhyme. It intensifies the impact of their words. In the example above, as in others like it, first you discover the pattern: **i** before **e** but just the opposite after **c**. But once you see it you would do much better spending some time then and there developing a little rhyme to remember it. You can make up front-end rhymes (**alliteration**) too: *Peter Piper picked a peck of pickled peppers.*

The first device, then, is **rhyme.**

2. Rhythm

Example

M I, crooked letter, crooked letter, I,
crooked letter, crooked letter, I P P I

An elementary student invented that trick to remember how to spell Mississippi. The **rhythm** method (*sic!*) is also used in the i-before-e verse above.

So the second device is **rhythm.**

3. Grouping

Example

Remember this number: 168221544

Response: Break it into subgroups (168 22 1544). That happens to be a Social Security number, and it is a lot easier to remember when it is broken into three smaller groups. If you practice saying it as follows, you are also using **rhythm**: One sixty-EIGHT pause Twenty-two pause One FIVE four four.

That's **grouping**.

In the following example, a sixth grader used all three devices:

M I S—Miss, S I S—sis, S I P—sip, P I—pi.

Rhyme, rhythm, and **grouping** are all **poetic** devices. All you have to remember, when the material seems appropriate, is to ask yourself if a little poem would help.

● To memorize "The Rhyme of the Ancient Mariner," "The Gettysburg Address," or a foreign language dialog, use **the grouping technique**. Once you understand the poem or speech, having read and thought about it enough, the next step is to break it into its meaningful parts. Master each unit in sequence, adding to what you already know and reviewing the remainder in each practice. The trick is to work in meaning units. Artificial breaks make no sense and don't stick. But if you remember *meaning*, the right words will flow along with that memory.

4. Coincidental Association

Example

Figure out a trick to remember that Fujiyama is 12365 feet high.

No? Space it like this: 12 365. That ought to remind you of the months and days of the year. It is pure coincidence, but, if you have the luck to stumble across such an association, you have it made. The world is full of them.

So add **coincidental association** to your bag of tricks.

When you are alert to them, coincidental associations pop up all over. Ask any name freak: Duhl, the math teacher; Grimm, the librarian. Or notice opposites: "Duhl is *not* dull" works just as well. "Mr. Hauser has a schnauzer."

The idea is to catch on to the new datum with a good hook, preferably several. Enrich the context, the meaning, from several angles. Coincidental association is something we all notice and enjoy naturally. For school work use it deliberately. Pennsylvania fits like a keystone in the thirteen original colonies. So it is the **keystone** state. Italy is shaped like a **boot.** The **principal** of a school is spelled **pal** and not **le** as in **principles** of chess. So the princi**pal** is always (or never) your **pal.** The **ie** in **piece? That's a pie**ce of **pie**. The spelling of **their, they're** and **there**? They all start with **the.**

5. Words from Other Words: Acronyms

Example

You know the five Great Lakes but are afraid you will forget them on the test. You need something to trigger your memory of their names. As you have learned, they are Ontario, Huron, Michigan, Superior, and Erie. Take the first letter of each, O H M S E, and rearrange them to spell some word. HOMES works. What are the names of the Great Lakes? Think of HOMES and you have it.

Words from the initial letters of other words are **acronyms.**

6. Coined Words

Example

You have to remember the colors of the visual spectrum: red, orange, yellow, green, blue, indigo, and violet. And you must remember them in order. Make up a name out of the initial letters: ROY G. BIV. It may be an inane name, but that will make it stick. On a recall test, all you have to do is write

R

O

Y

G

B

I

V

and then fill in the word for each letter.

As you can see, **coined words** are a kind of acronym.

7. Sentence

Example

The lines of the musical scale? You know they are E G B D F but are afraid you might forget. **Every Good Boy Does Fine** always worked, didn't it?

A made-up **sentence** is still a good device.

8. Story

Example

If necessary, the sentence can be expanded into a story. You have to remember the twelve cranial nerves in order: olfactory, optic, oculomotor, trochlear, trigeminal, abducens, facial, auditory, glossopharyngeal, vagus, accessory, and hypoglossal. Which device would give you the most assurance of retrieval, something like **rhythm and grouping,** or perhaps a **sentence,** or a **story**? Thus, for **rhythm and grouping** the terms might be arranged with emphasis and pauses like this:

> olfactory, optic, OCULOMOTOR
> trochlear, trigeminal, ABDUCENS
> facial, auditory, GLOSSOPHARYNGEAL
> vagus, accessory, HYPOGLOSSAL

But make a **sentence** from the initial letters of each of the terms and on top of that make it into a verse and you have more likelihood of retrieval. There are more **links**:

> On old Olympus' towering top
> a fat-assed German vaults and hops.

But even better would be a **story** and better than that, one in which **the words chosen sound like the terms to be remembered:**

> At the **oil factory** (olfactory) the **optician**
> (optic) looked for the **occupant** (oculomotor)
> of the **truck** (trochlear). And so on.

From Gordon H. Bower, *Psychology Today*, October 1973.

The extra imagination required of you and the increased involvement pay off in deeper memory traces. You will discover that a story is more efficient in the long run. Once you are familiar with the list, creating a story forces you to pay attention to the terms, their spelling, their pronunciation, and similarities with other words. You can't be passive. Obviously, **connecting, rephrasing,** and **paying attention** are all required.

When you think about it, all the methods mentioned thus far are based on **association** of some sort, associating the thing to be remembered with things already known or catchy. When you call to mind the one, the other is tied to it and comes up, too. **Association** could just as well be called **connecting** or **linking** or **organizing** or **webbing**.

- **General Technique: Association**

Following are some elaborations and some additional linking techniques often used by memory experts. They take more initial effort, but they also last longer.

9. Link Method

Example

You have eight words to remember in order:

match	blackboard
ivy	mug
big toe	acorn
bacon	painting

Make a story by doing something a little kooky with each item and then linking it firmly to the next item. Go on from item to item in this manner until you use them up. A sample story is given below. As you read it, visualize each item in its context. Then recall the story and see if you can list the items in order:

A giant **match** *is strolling in an* **ivy** *patch. The ivy starts twining around his* **big toe**. *He spies a slab of* **bacon** *and hurriedly rubs it on his toe to keep the ivy from clinging. But he is so upset he leaps from the patch, still carrying the bacon. He hangs it on a* **blackboard** *set up in the open meadow. Why is it there? He notices there is a shaving* **mug** *fastened to the center and a ceramic* **acorn** *as big as an apple sticking out of it. Then he sees an artist* *seated nearby and realizes the whole thing is the subject of a surreal* **painting**.

Don't look back. Try to recall the story and see if you can picture the eight items as you go along.

If you do have trouble remembering, chances are you were passive when you read it. As you know, you must be alert and actively paying attention to meaning. Who could blame you? It wasn't your own story, so you didn't get a chance to put it in your own words.

So make up *your own* **story** for the next eight words. You will probably score 100 per cent this time. Just remember to make a connection you can visualize between each pair. Don't be afraid to let it be bizarre, the moreso the better.

candy	razor
bee	sailor
typewriter	Buddha
love	footnote

You can see why making up a little story in this manner can be called a **linking method**. It has the advantage that **you need work with only two items at a time**. You don't have to worry that earlier items will fade. In recall, you can start with any item and move forward or backward along the chain, each item calling up the image of the next. And, of course, you have to be active, put it in your own words, and connect items according to your own inner guidance. It is *your* story.

The **link method** may seem a needlessly round about way of remembering things. You may not like silly stories. And you may think you have no imagination for such things and begin to sweat when you think you have to make one up. But one evening's practice of four or five sets of words at home—where you are safe—will make you a convert. You will see that in half an hour's time you can remember four or five sets of words totaling thirty or forty *in order* and perfectly. Not only that but the next day you can still remember them! For most readers that is a unique experience.

● **A Chain**

If you prefer, you can skip making up a story and just concentrate on creating a powerful connection between each pair as you go down the list, dropping one and adding another each time. With just a little practice you can master fifty to 100 or more in any one chain. Think how great that will be for mastering anatomy terms or for the periodic table.Don't forget, visual images make a deeper impression than do abstract concepts. Use the strange or wonderful whenever you can.

For long lists, **the link method** is one of the most effective.

10. *Method of Places*

Example

You have to remember ten grocery items to buy at the store but can't find a pencil:

lettuce	toilet paper
butter	sugar
pork roast	honey
milk	potatoes
cornflakes	fly swatter

If you try to memorize this list, as most people would, just by going over it again and again, chances are you won't remember most of them. How *can* you remember them? One way is to imagine them located in various spots throughout your house along some route you usually take, perhaps from the time you get out of bed to the time you go out the front door.

Be sure to exaggerate or use the bizarre. Here is an example:

As I put my feet over the edge of the bed and onto the floor, I'm shocked by cold, slimy, slippery lumps where my slippers should be. Two decaying heads of **lettuce** *have taken their place. I slog to the bathroom, an awkward lettuce lump on each foot. I squeeze the toothpaste tube but get* **butter** *instead of Fluorident. At the foot of the back stairs, wavering in delicate balance on the newel post is a gigantic* **pork roast** *topped off with a pork-pie hat and a sardonic grin. I struggle to the kitchen. When I pour a glass of* **milk** *out come* **cornflakes** *instead. I hurry to the hall closet for my coat. Hundreds of rolls of* **toilet paper** *tumble out knocking me down. I go through the dining room and find a blanket of snow. But it isn't snow; it's* **sugar** *everywhere. There must be 200 pounds of it. In the living room, my wife, waiting to kiss me goodbye, turns in my arms into a five-foot-eight jar of* **honey**. *The foyer is blocked by a* **potato** *man I shoulder out of my way, only to discover swarms of flies coming down the stairwell after the sticky honey on my clothes from my encounter in the living room. Wearily, I reach for a* **fly swatter** *leaning against the hall tree and begin swatting away.*

Of course, this is not your house, and you probably don't have much motivation to remember this particular list. But if you skim over it, you will see how the **method of places** works.

The **method of places** has been in continuous use since the time of Greek orators who didn't have cue cards. The orator would picture the layout of a familiar place, his home perhaps. He would imagine himself moving from place to place in that dwelling and putting one item in each place as he went along. "In the first place," the foyer, maybe, he put his first point, and "in the second place," perhaps his courtyard, he put the next major point, and so on. He could use the same structure for each new speech, storing his key ideas in the spaces as he moved along.

11. The Grid Method: Place and Link Combined

It was inevitable that the place and link methods would be combined and streamlined. The **grid method** has room for fifty-four or more items. Re-usable nine-square grids replace your bathroom, kitchen, foyer, and so on. Picture yourself in the doorway of a large cubeshaped room. Start with the floor. It is laid out in nine large squares like this:

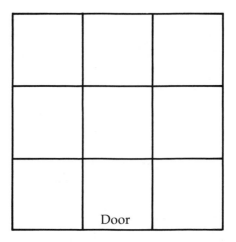

Here are your first nine items of a list of fifty you have to remember in order:

hat	hawk
fountain pen	curtain
ring	baby
bicycle	horse
gin	

Put your first item, the **hat** , in the far left corner. Put the **pen** in the next square and invent a visual connection. Maybe the **pen** is alive and decides to wear the **hat**:

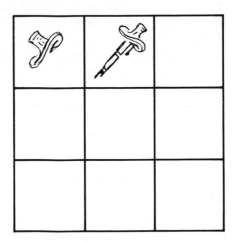

Then go on and link the **pen** in square 2 with the **ring** in square 3. Then the ring with the **bicycle** in square 4:

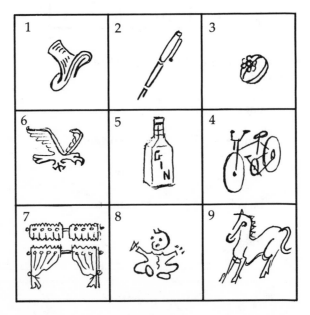

*The **pen** slaps the **hat** on his head and turns to square 3
where he sees a diamond **ring** so large he could wear it for a
belt. The big ring gleaming brightly around his middle, he
sees the **bicycle** in square 4 and despite his inexperience
pedals it clumsily into square 5 where he smashes into a
three-foot **gin** bottle standing in as a hydrant. Gin spouts
into the air and into square 6 where an alcoholic **hawk**
swoops and guzzles. The hawk careens crazily and crashes,
tangling himself in a lacy **curtain** draped on a limb in
square 7. This wakes the **baby** on the grass nearby in square
8, and his wails frighten the grazing **horse** in square 9 who
gallops out of the scene.*

Note: This story is more elaborate than necessary. For example, once you
have linked the pen and hat, you can forget the hat when you link the pen and
ring. The ring can become the front wheel of the bicycle and you can ignore the
hat and pen. Nevertheless, when you picture the hat in square 1, the pen in
square 2 will come to mind, and the pen will trigger the ring.

You can place your next nine items on the back wall in a
similar grid and then go on to the other three walls and the
ceiling. You can then go next door to an enclosed squash court
and pick up fifty-four more spaces. Then go on to the gym.
This expandable method affords as many spaces as you are
likely to need and gets easier to use with each new list.

12. Peg-Word Method

Instead of places, as in the nine-square grid, you can
memorize some object to take the place of each digit from 1 to
10. **One** is a **gun,** 2 is a **shoe,** and so on. You can attach each
to-be-remembered item to a **peg.** If **cornflakes** is to be remembered as your second item, picture **cornflakes** associated with a
shoe (for 2). The shoe is full of cornflakes. "What's my second
item? Well, 2 is a shoe. Oh, yes. Cornflakes."

Maintain a **peg** for each digit. (**Three** is a **tree,** 4 is a **door,** 5
is a **hive,** 6 is a **stick.**) Your own pegs will stick better. Rhyme
will help, too. Once memorized, the pegs are available for repeated use. The pegs are saved. You can hang new lists on
them as needed. Random items are hard to remember, and

numbers are, too. Images are much easier. So the **peg method is popular.**

13. Digit-Consonant System: Pegs for Long Lists or for Numbers

Suppose you want to remember the Billboard Hot One Hundred *in order*. They change every week. Or you are a checker in a supermarket and have a whole new list of specials each week. Or, more to the point here, you want to remember 100 facts for a biology quiz and next week 200 for art history. You will be taking hundreds of tests during college. The following 100-word peg system—learned once only in one short evening—will serve you over and over throughout college. It looks complicated until you catch on, but hang in there. Once you examine the list, you will see it has built into it some easy to remember memory tags. For anyone willing to devote an evening to it, this system is well worth the time. It can save your life again and again.

The system is called a *digit-consonant system* and has been around for several centuries. Here is one version. You will have to be a little patient. Once you try a few examples, it will all fall into place. If you decide to give it a try, it is a job you have to do only once.

To begin with, each digit, 1 to 0, is associated with a consonant sound. The *sound* of the consonant is what counts. K*at* or c*at* would do just as well in this system. And the vowels don't matter; they are just spacers. Here are your basic building blocks:

1 t, d	6 sh, j, ch
2 n	7 ng, k, g
3 m	8 f, v
4 r	9 b, p
5 l	0 s, z

Let's play with the consonants assigned to the digits and see how they can be converted into words. Suppose you want a peg to stand for 92 or maybe you just want to remember 92 for some reason. In our chart **b** or **p** always represents **9**, and **n always represents 2**. So I have, say, **p n**. I can put in *any* vowel that suits me. I will use **a**, and my word is **pan**. The digits represented by **pan** are **9** and **2**, or **92**. As you can see, you could work out a word for any number, and you could use the sounds assigned to the basic ten digits to build your Social Security number, your car license, history dates. Since words you can visualize are easier to remember than abstract ideas, use vivid nouns whenever you can.

THE ONE-HUNDRED-WORD LIST

If you had built earlier a system of, say, 100 pegs, all based on the consonants for those first ten digits, you could then use them as pegs to hang any hundred to-be-remembered facts. Suppose one of the facts I have to remember is **cherry** and it is the ninety-second item on my list. My peg for **92** that I worked out is **pan**. So I picture a frying **pan** filled with one giant **cherry**. On the test, I say to myself, "What was my ninety-second item? Let's see. The peg works out as **pan**." [You would have used your system enough that the word **pan** would probably come automatically, but if necessary you could reconstruct it from the basic digit-consonants.] The recall process would go like this:

92 —→ pan —→ —→ cherry.

What word could stand for 58? That would have to be l—f from the chart. Fill in any old vowel(s): **leaf.**

For **64** the first letter would be **sh**, **j**, or **ch**. And the **4** is **r**. So a word for **64** would be **ch r** . **Chair** would do.

A word for 77? Something like **coke** or **kong** would do. Notice **c** or **k** gives the /k/ sound we need. Spelling doesn't count.

And 23? **Name.**

Remembering Numbers

You can use this system for dates, phone numbers, zip codes. Zip code 59922 could be **Lebbanon** (with an extra **b**, of course).

This, then, is the idea on which the **digit-consonant system** is based.

Memorizing the List

Note the configurations of the letters associated with 1. The **t** and **d** have *one* vertical line. For digit 2 the **n** has *two* vertical lines. You can remember the **r** for 4 because **four** has an **r** in it. Flip the **b** or **p** for the digit 9 and they will look like 9. You can figure out a memory cue for each of the first ten digits. So, if you should forget the consonant for some digit, you could use your memory device to recall it. With a consonant system, there is a tie with the digit. Other peg systems are not so easy to remember.

Expanding the Basic Digit-Consonant List

Now for the Billboard Hot One Hundred. With just the basic ten digit-consonants, you can easily build nine more groups of ten with built-in memory cues. That is, you really don't have to learn ninety more items, because you use combinations of the already-learned consonants. It will probably take you less than an hour to memorize the list that follows. If you do, it will be yours for your four years in college. You can use it over and over to remember any list of facts for any course.

Take a good look at the first nine words. Notice each can have only one consonant sound taken from the basic chart. (All but the sixth start with **h** because **h** is not a consonant sound.) Starting With number 10, we need two consonant sounds. So **d** for 1 begins the next ten numbers. If you look at the end sound, you will see that each comes from the original ten. Numbers 20 through 29 all begin with an /n/ sound for 2. Look at each group of ten that follows and you will see a beautiful

ONE HUNDRED DIGIT-CONSONANT PEGS

1 hat	30 mouse	60 juice	90 pizza
2 hen	31 mat	61 jet	91 pot
3 ham	32 moon	62 gin	92 pen
4 hair	33 mom	63 jam	93 poem
5 hill	34 mare	64 jar	94 pear
6 shoe	35 mail	65 jail	95 pail
7 hook	36 match	66 judge	96 patch
8 hoof	37 mug	67 jack	97 pick
9 hoop	38 muff	68 jove	98 puff
	39 map	69 ship	99 pipe
10 dice			100 doses
11 deed	40 rice	70 goose	
12 down	41 road	71 gate	
13 dam	42 rain	72 gun	
14 deer	43 ram	73 gum	
15 doll	44 roar	74 gear	
16 dish	45 rail	75 gale	
17 deck	46 rich	76 gash	
18 dove	47 rock	77 kick	
19 dope	48 roof	78 goof	
	49 rope	79 cab	
20 nose			
21 knot	50 lace	80 face	
22 nun	51 lady	81 foot	
23 name	52 lawn	82 fan	
24 near	53 loom	83 foam	
25 nail	54 liar	84 fire	
26 niche	55 lily	85 file	
27 neck	56 lash	86 fish	
28 knife	57 lock	87 fig	
29 knob	58 leaf	88 fife	
	59 lip	89 fob	

Modified from M. N. Young and W. B. Gibson. *How to develop an exceptional memory*. Hollywood: Wilshire Book Company, 1962.

regularity and simplicity, all the words building on the original ten sounds. In case you forget, it is easy to recall. Any peg in the fifty series is going to begin with an /l/ sound. Any in the eighty series, with an /f/ sound. The second consonant sound for numbers composed of two digits will progress in order through the basic sounds: /d/ or /t/ for 1, /n/ for 2, /m/ for 3, and so on.

Is It Worth Your Time?

Some people can't bear this sort of work. If they have ways of remembering masses of facts and those ways are more suited to their personality and nature, by all means they should use them. However, a half hour or so in your freshman year mastering a basic system like this will solve many problems for you throughout college. It is like learning the ABC's or the typewriter keyboard. It is a one-time-only chore.

Review

These memory strategies are already fading from your mind. If you do something else right now, the memory trace will fade even quicker. The longer you delay in refreshing your learning, the greater the memory loss. By tomorrow your recall could be as little as ten per cent.

How can you stop this memory loss? Experiments show that a few minutes of reinforcing at the end of a learning session will save you from having to redo the whole thing later. A good reinforcing session right away with occasional touch ups is the swiftest way through school work.

Reviewing these thirteen memorizing methods can be accomplished in a couple of minutes. Try grouping them in meaningful bunches. That will make the job manageable. Counting helps: There are thirteen methods listed. How were they presented? From the simpler devices like rhyme to structured, more efficient plans like the digit-consonant system.

How about some logical subgroups?

Rhyme, rhythm, and **grouping** seem to go together as **poetic** devices.

Coincidental association we will set off by itself. It seems to precede more intentional associations.

Acronyms, coined words, sentences, and **stories** seem to fit together as **grammatical** devices, going from simple to complex.

We can put the **link method** by itself. Actually linking goes on in sentences and stories as well as the four techniques that follow.

The **method of places,** the **grid, peg-word,** and **digit-consonant** systems are all **location** techniques, simple to complex again.

Thus,

> **poetic** (three devices)
> **coincidental association** (one)
> **grammatical** (four techniques)
> **link method** (one)
> **location** (four techniques)

So the cumbersome memory problem of thirteen separate items can be reduced to five or fewer bunches of *meaningfully* related ideas. And all these are arranged within their own groups from simpler to more complex. Your own groupings could be quite different from these, depending on what relationships you see among them.

Just examining the list in such a manner is already a big step toward remembering. It doesn't take long, and it makes more sense to the observer, because it is his own sense. He created the groupings and the relationships himself. His own inner thought patterns have been thrown like a net over those in the book, and both are now somewhat different. He has rephrased the material for his own unique comprehension.

Now see how much you can recall. Then take a break. Below are samples. Name the memory technique each represents. Use your own words if ours don't come to mind. After you have supplied all you can, leaf through this section and fill in the rest. Some of the samples may represent more than one technique.

1   **i** before **e** except after **c** . . .

2   One sixty-EIGHT pause
&   twenty-two pause
3   one FIVE four four

4   Fuji's height, 12365 feet,
    has the same digits as the
    twelve months and the 365 days
    of the year.

5   H — Huron
    O — Ontario
    M — Michigan
    E — Erie
    S — Superior

6   ROY G BIV to remember the
    colors of the visual spectrum.

7   Lines of the musical scale:
    Every **G**ood **B**oy **D**oes **F**ine.

8   At the **oil factory** the **optician**
    looked for the **occupant** of the
    truck: olfactory, optic, oculo-
    motor, trochlear.

9   A giant **match** is strolling in
    an **ivy** patch. The ivy starts
    twining around his **big toe** . . . .

10   **Butter** in the toothpaste tube,
     pork roast on the newel post,
     toilet paper in the hall closet . . . .

11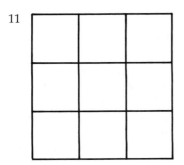

12   Three is a **tree**,
     four is a **door** . . .

13   **Lip** stands for 59.

FURTHER AIDS

Reinforce

After a session of learning, memorizing, and reviewing—
once you develop the knack, it will take far less time than most
grinds spend on studying—it is vital to reinforce your memory
traces within a few hours to a day later. Otherwise they fade
and you have to redo your work.

TEST YOURSELF

"Let's see. How many groups did I make for those thirteen
memory techniques? Oh, yes. Five. The bunches contain . . . ?
Oh, yes: 3, 1, 4, 1, 4 techniques each. First group? Poetic:
Rhyme, rhythm, grouping . . . ." And so forth. Go back and
rework the items you can't recall. Do it again the next day.

Three or four days later review again for a minute or two, then every week or so till the test.

USE FLASH CARDS

You probably used flash cards in grade school. They work just as well in college for foreign language vocabulary, dates and events, formulas and their meanings. After a learning session, make up a pack of cards to carry with you. Rehearse while waiting for a bus or standing in line for a movie. But remember, only a few minutes at a time. The new context and the different time often cause new memory links. Short, intense practices are best. Rehearsal works only when your mind is fresh and attentive.

● **Be sure to overlearn.** A few extra rounds make all the difference in the amount you will retain.

● **Once a card is learned, take it out of the pack.** When you use up the pack, start a new one.

Make an Analogy

Analogy means comparing one thing with another. In memorizing, it means looking at the new thing and asking What is this like that I already know? New, difficult material can be made familiar through analogy. For example, students compare the flow of electricitythrough a wire with the flow of water through a pipe. Voltage, current, and resistance compare with water pressure, amount of flow, and size of pipe. The simplified scheme of the water analogy provides a working model and can be developed into a more sophisticated model.

It is worth the effort to toy with some hard-to-remember concept until it reminds you of some familiar structure. Often it will be some common experience or observation from nature. Once you make the connection, you are home free. Analogy is the most powerful tool of thought. Try it every chance you get.

Develop Assurance

If you want to improve your memory, be confident. That may sound a bit ridiculous. But that is what happened when you learned to ride a bicycle or drive a car, isn't it? At first you did it awkwardly, but the more you practiced the surer you were. The activity had changed from a set of awkward rules to nerve-ending responses. You had it on your finger tips.

A while back I had each student in class learn the first and last names of everyone else—all in one fifty-minute period. I had never done this before myself, and I was expected to perform when everyone else had finished. There I was encouraging everyone while I was getting sweaty hands and developing considerable anxiety. What if the teacher failed? It was hard, but I did manage with one or two mistakes. But after that session it got easier and easier. Now I am absolutely sure I can do it with 120 students each semester. That is 240 bits of information. Not only that but I am not at all worried. No sweaty palms. The less anxiety the better I perform. That is the point. Success makes you more confident, and confidence makes it easier to succeed.

So try it till you succeed. Then try a few more times just to convince yourself.

Key: Practice.

Have some fun with memorizing. Make a game of it. Try it out in non-stress situations whenever you get a chance. Persistence will pay off in better grades and an easy mind.

> *In a Nutshell*
>
> **Reinforce**
> **Test yourself**
> **Use flash cards**
> **Overlearn**
> **Make an analogy**
> **Develop assurance: Persist**
> **Key: Practice**

RECALL STRATEGIES: HOW TO FIND IT AGAIN

Memory as System

Memory is a system, not a junk pile. If you put it in a good place to begin with and have a good cross-referencing system, you will be able to find what you filed away. It is 'memorized' when it is well placed. The trick is to think of memory as a filing system, not the hall closet.

Remembering and Problem Solving

As you will see in later chapters, remembering is really problem solving. When you analyze how you do the two things, it is the same approach: What am I being asked? Is it possible for me to get the answer? (Is it stored there in the first place?) Where will I find it? How?

A structure from which to retrieve stuff is crucial. It is true that time-lapse and rehearsal frequency can affect retention, but it depends on how the time is used and what kind of rehearsal. Once these conditions are met, how do you get it back?

You have to put together information you can find; you have to see what the combination yields and go on from there; and you go about it in an orderly way. You actually apply systematic rules, though you probably are not conscious of them, whenever you try to find something in your memory banks.

Some part of ourselves knows immediately whether or not even to try. We seem to know before we even start whether the search is futile. When asked, "Where were you a week ago?" we know somehow that we were *somewhere*. But, next, can we actually recover the information? Often our minimal expectations of ourselves are such that we don't even try. And often we give up too soon. Experience can alter our attitude.

The greater the persistence duration, the greater the chance of success.

What did you have yesterday for dinner? Most people would tackle that. What were you doing Tuesday afternoon two weeks ago? Many would give up on that, but with encouragement and prompting almost everyone would recover the information. What were you doing on Valentine's Day three years ago? Impossible? With persistence and conscious search procedures there is a good chance you can recall this information, too.

If you feel you *can* make reasonable decisions, if you can guide your own life, if you can function well as a cook or carpenter, then you should have no trouble remembering either. It is exactly the same mechanism, but you may not realize it.

Retrieval Processes

How do we go about it? We know we don't just punch in the question and out comes the answer. It is much more involved. Who are you? Even a question as basic as that requires interpretation. Should I even answer? Should I give a false answer? What is actually being asked? My name, my occupation, my authority, my social class? If a Zen priest or a Socrates asks, I may decide I don't have an acceptable answer; I don't know. Nevertheless, almost instantly I can select from all the possible answers and respond appropriately. (Sometimes I misunderstand and give the wrong answer.)

Other kinds of questions may require elaborate search procedures. If you can spare half an hour or so, observe your thought processes as you try to remember what you were doing on Valentine's Day three years ago. Work your way through the problem out loud—into a cassette if possible. Or write it down. What steps do you observe? What strategies?

Go on reading when you are ready.

If you are typical, though no one says you have to be, you

didn't try to get the answer all at once. You probably bit off a smaller piece, a subgroup first:

> *What day of the week was the 14th? If it was a school day, that would narrow it down. Let's see: This year it's Tuesday, so it was Sunday if leap year doesn't throw it off. . . . It doesn't, so it was Sunday. That's tougher. School schedules and classes would have been easier to reconstruct. Okay, forget that. We usually celebrate the date. Did I give Ruth that heart-shaped paper weight? No, that was later on. But I had it then and put it away because I had something else for her. What? That delicate gold heart pendant. Can't visualize the situation, though. Would the girls have been home? No. Kathy was in Chico, Patty in Santa Rosa. Aha! We drove to Chico Saturday. Kathy had received the soap we sent. After all that driving, probably didn't go anywhere Sunday. Was I downstairs writing a haiku to go with the gift? School work? Reading journals maybe. I wasn't chairman that year. . . .*

And so on. Was your process similar? There is some subgrouping, some looping back to prior questions, and moving ahead again. I try to **reconstruct the setting**. I look for **contexts** or **associations that may yield the answer. I get lots more information than I actually need, more than was included in the briefer version above. This helps me visualize** the scene in which the information is stored. Later on I thought about other Valentine's Days before and after, for **contrast** and **triggering.** Also I explored how I was **feeling** at that time, **my emotions.** Gradually more and more of the picture is filled in. When I can't find the answer, I work on smaller parts and try again.

Lots of tries are blind alleys. But I begin to feel it is possible that I really can find the answer. This sparks my enthusiasm. I sharpen up my questions and strengthen my persistence. Now I am really going to try for that answer. I use both **logic** and **hunches.**

I play with possibilities. I reason with myself.

No doubt these steps seem perfectly reasonable to you. When we are not panicked, we use them. It is often fun. The trouble is we forget all about them if we are in a chemistry exam and we sit there like jerks. As you can see, we have lots of avenues to explore.

Could you remember the names of all the people in your high school class? It has been found that for such a task **persistence** does pay off. The longer people stick to it, for days and days and sometimes even months, the more they can remember.

Thus, we do have strategies within us for retrieval. We don't have to throw up our hands and hope for lightning to strike. Even if I don't know Napoleon's birth date, I can use this process to narrow down the possible dates considerably. On a multiple-choice test that could be close enough. And we can throw these recall strategies into play deliberately.

ELEVEN RETRIEVAL STRATEGIES

As you know, to trigger recall we must loop and detour as needed. Don't try to remember these strategies word for word. Just take time to familiarize yourself with them. See if you do use them. Then during tests, allow yourself the freedom to make use of whatever approach is needed.

- **Persist.** If you have the time, use it. One or two points could raise your grade. In retrieval, persistence works.

- **Play. Treat it as a game.** That reduces anxiety, and that in turn frees your mind to seek alternatives.

- **Divide the question into smaller questions.** "If I figure out B, that may lead to C, and together they may yield A."

- **Rephrase the original question.** Go back from time

to time; see how you are doing; try another path.

● **Reconstruct a setting or several settings.** Search the setting for clues. They may lead to other groupings that may contain the answer.

● **Use left-overs.** Recalled contexts usually contain more details than actually needed. Scan them for accidental aids.

● **Visualize.** A recalled scene can be held before your mind's eye while you examine it for information. Be willing to suspend your search while you stroll around looking.

● **Use your own analogy.** The formula relating voltage, current, and resistence? Trace out the water analogy. State the relations. Based on this, reconstruct the formula.

● **Try alternatives.** At blind alleys back up and try a new path. Realize there are dozens of ways to skin a cat.

● **Feel free to back up, defer, move ahead, relax, and get intense as needed.** If a path is temporarily blocked, set the question aside. Do some other parts of the problem. Then come back to it.

● **Use both logic and hunches.** Memory is a tease. Both rhyme and reason are needed to woo her.

It is not necessary to slave over these strategies. As you can see, you have already used them; they are part of everyone's thinking processes. So just become conscious of them. Get the feel of them and carry away the assurance that you do have all these tactics already. And trust yourself to put them to work at the right time.

TROUBLE SHOOTING

If you forget and it hurts, go ahead and feel sorry for yourself for a minute, but then analyze what happened. Or do you like losing? Only about three things can interfere with remembering:

Panic
Wrong Filing Strategies
Wrong Recall Tactics

There are remedies for each.

● **Panic** Panic is fear of the unknown or insecurity, lack of confidence. Beforehand, you can reduce its likelihood by doing dry runs. First, of course, get the stuff into your memory banks using the suggestions in this chapter. But then do some confidence building. Don't exaggerate the importance of this school game. No test score measures your character or worth. It is just like a game of basketball. So get rid of the power over you that you allow the test to have.

Better still, practice remembering in the same way and in the same sort of environment as the test itself. Make up test questions like your teacher uses. Check out the territory in advance. Find out all you can from the teacher about the kind of test he gives; talk to his former students. Analyze his old tests if you can get hold of any. It is money in the bank.

Practice the stress situation until you are used to it. It is just like learning to drive. (More on getting test-wise in Chapter Two.)

● **Wrong Filing Strategies** When you get your test back, do an item analysis. Go back and see where and how you filed the item. Figure out if you could have anticipated this problem. If you did try to file it but it didn't stick, see if you left out any of the general rules:

Pay attention.
Rephrase.
Organize.

Whatever happened, you will be ready next time.

A Tip The failure may not be your fault—at least not the first time. Memory is not literal. That is, a good memory digests ideas, not exact wording. If your teacher tests verbatim, word-for-word recall, your first quiz will show that. In that case, your only recourse is to apply one of the thirteen memory devices in this chapter or some other you invent. That is the game and you might as well arm yourself. The general rules will store the material for you, and the memory devices will bring back the data verbatim.

● **Wrong Recall Tactics**   If item analysis reveals you did file the material well, you may simply need to brush up your recall tactics. Next time, when you reach a brick wall, do easy questions until you are calm again. Then come back and put your strategies to work. Treat the search as a game and have some fun with it. After all, school is not the only game in town. If you flunk out, it could be the best thing that ever happened to you. So relax. To be free to play with alternatives, you can't let panic immobilize you. Try associations, tangents, clues in other questions on the test, rephrasing and so forth. Persist till they throw you out of the room. Play to win.

SUMMARY

Skilled memory tactics influence grades tremendously, much more than most students or even most teachers realize. Though most courses claim higher goals, **what is remembered is what gets graded.** It is difficult to teach how to use facts and how to generate new structures. It is harder to test such learning. So everyone settles for the easier practice of checking up on memory. It would be honest and fair to say so, but no one will admit it. Many are sincere, often well schooled, and even nice guys.

Meanwhile there are grades to get. Knowledge that one can cope can make school much more bearable. And there is a bright side to memory training, too. Tactics that help one get good grades are not limited to school games. A good memory system is a data-processing system. Such processing is a fundamental kind of thinking. Strategies needed to get good grades are exactly those needed for educating oneself.

Thus, as Piaget and others have suggested, our understanding is limited to the completeness of our field of vision.

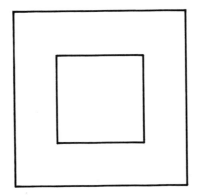

If we step back, we see a larger picture. a clearer, more complete one. This seems to be what happens when we assimilate new information. Our view grows from a simple whole to a more detailed and complex whole, always integrated.

The memory strategies outlined in this chapter are in harmony with this kind of growth.

2

Raising Test Scores

IN THIS CHAPTER

SYNOPSIS

Testing is one more aspect of the school game without real meaning beyond the classroom door. About the only thing you can be sure a test measures is *test-taking skill*. Knowledge of the elements of this game and the rules for playing will raise grades and reduce anxiety. Players use exactly the same general approach as they do for memorizing and retrieving information.

This chapter begins with some research findings on tests and their limitations and provides an overview of how tests work, together with four basic rules of the game. A sample test for you to take follows and then an item analysis. From this analysis are distilled fifteen test-taking tips. These in turn boil down to the Chapter One general rules: Pay attention, rephrase, and connect. Taking a test is a retrieval problem.

Next is a general discussion of test-awareness including the general rule: *Analyze missed items out loud*. Five common errors in test taking and six techniques for gaining know-how follow.

Then come examples and analyses for various objective tests (multiple choice, true-false, matching, sentence-completion, critical analysis, and analogy) and tips for handling each type. A section on taking essay tests gives rules and strategies and a method for breaking through mental blocks and for answering questions you think you can't answer.

The chapter then tells the best test-taking attitude, whether or not to cram, how to review for a test, and how much to study. The next section tells how to overcome any problems likely to occur before, during and after a test, including how to turn a failing score to your advantage.

The same problem-solving approach as outlined in Chapter One emphasizes the fact that test-analysis is a genuine educational activity with application to real-life problems in general.

THE LIMITATIONS OF TESTS

Although tests seem deeply embedded in the system, there is no sense in granting them power over our lives. It is not difficult to keep them in their place. In fact, if not taken seriously, they can be entertaining diversions. But a good gamesman plays to win. Otherwise, why play? It is a matter of focusing one's attention on the elements and rules of the game.

Effect of Test-Taking Skills on Grades

Next to memory skill, knowing how to take tests has the most direct effect on grades. As little as fifteen to twenty per cent of your grade will be for what you know. The rest reflects your test-taking know-how. *Grade-point average is affected more by test-taking dexterity than by just about anything else you could name.* But, as you well know, along with memory techniques, it is one of the least taught skills. Learning how tests work and discovering how to take them can make the difference between a C and an A score. That has been demonstrated in many experiments. Perhaps that is why schools give so little help in test-taking. Aware students could wreck the curve. Practice in the right techniques can even change your IQ score.[1] Test taking is a skill like any other and can be learned. As you will see, much of what you need to know is common sense. If you don't already know it, the information you will find here can change your test scores significantly. In fact, you will probably know more than most teachers do about what a test actually measures, how it is put together, where its weak points are, and how to get a high score with no more knowledge than you usually have.

What Tests Really Measure

It is naive to think that good test scores reflect anything important. A high score shows only one thing: *Test-taking skill.* Basing grades on tests is about as sensible as granting a driver's license to someone who knows how many traffic lights there are on Main Street.[2] It is a rare teacher whose tests actually measure his long-term goals. Studies show no relation between test scores and subject mastery and no relation with one's future success.[3] High scores often simply show that the student

[1] See Arthur Whimbey, "You Can Learn to Raise Your IQ Score," *Psychology Today*, January 1976.

[2] Jennings and Nathan.

[3] See Robert Glaser, "Ten Untenable Assumptions of College Instruction," *Educational Record* , Spring 1968. See also Jennings and Nathan.

has had prior experience. He may be neither smarter nor more apt than someone to whom the course is brand new. He may have learned the answers before he signed up for the course. So a good score may actually reflect the least learning.

A good score may simply reflect speed. (Is the ability to do things fast listed as a goal in any courses you have taken?) Timed objective tests ignore differences in the way people learn and in their biological clocks.

As plenty of studies show, a good score does not mean you will remember. Neither is it a good predictor of performance or of success in a field of study.[4]

Course grades tell neither what a student knows nor what he can do.[5]

A typical objective test (essay tests are usually objective tests with words strung between the facts) is a poor way to measure anything worthwhile.[6]

Errors in Interpreting Results

Individual test items vary widely (*wildly*) in level of thinking required, but items are usually weighted the same. It is conceivable that a student could answer all the thought questions and miss all the fact questions. A jerk could do the opposite and come with the same score. As William G. Perry notes, "Intelligence tests require thought, but generally in little spurts and restricted operations that are incapable of revealing its larger outlines. Questionnaires prohibit thought by setting precast alternatives and forbidding the respondent to say how he would form the question and qualify the answer."[7] To get any sense out of a score, an item-by-item analysis for each student would have to be made. A simple raw score means nothing.[8]

And what about one's "wrong" answers? As research shows, without a conversation with the student about his reasoning on each item, a teacher has no idea of what influenced

[4] Jennings and Nathan.
[5] Glaser.
[6] Jennings and Nathan.
[7] William G. Perry, Jr., *Forms of Intellectual and Ethical Development in the College Years*, New York: Holt, Rinehart, and Winston, 1968.
[8] Ruth.

the answer.[9] A "right" answer could be so shaky or so illogically arrived at as to be useless. Right/wrong testing ignores complex reasoning processes.[10] And so on. The more we examine what can go wrong in making, giving, interpreting, and *taking* a written test, the more we see its limitations. Most damning of all, objective tests contain up to four-fifths wrong information. No respectable learning theory can endorse a stacked deck of such proportions. Imagine trying to teach golf by showing four times out of five the wrong way to do it.

Even expensively researched and carefully controlled standardized tests are subject to all these dangers—as test makers themselves readily admit. Their attempts to persuade school people to recognize test limitations have met with little success.[11]

HOW TESTS WORK: THE TESTING GAME

The following analysis and rules-of-the-game are adapted from a paper on testing by expert test-taker and test-analyst Karl Staubach.[12]

Analysis of the Test Game

● **Motives.** Find out your opponent's motives, and while you are at it, know your own.

● **Competition.** Test makers want to rank test takers. They deliberately leave out questions everyone gets right. That throws players into competition with each other. There is no escape. A high score for you means a low score for someone else.

---

[9] Jennings and Nathan.
[10] Ruth.
[11] Ruth.
[12] Diablo Valley College, Pleasant Hill, California.

● **Artificial Grading.** When tests compare students with each other, the grades are artificial. A teacher or test maker can set the cut-off points anywhere he pleases. "I'm getting too many A's. I'm going to set the cut-off at 95 instead of 90." And there goes your head. "I made the test too tough. I'm going to lower the A cut-off to 65." "Too many students are getting high scores on the entrance exams. We'll have to raise the cut-off score." On every test someone decides to *invent* the grade categories. The categories are *not* God-given.

● **Failure and Guilt.** Another requirement of the game is to make your right answer correspond to the testor's. False, incorrect, unsatisfactory, or wrong answers are *bad* answers. And you should be ashamed of yourself!

● **Look Alikes.** One fascinating observation from research is that students whose work is most similar to that of their instructor get the best grades.[13] Naturally people who already see things the way the teacher does have less to learn from him. Thus, students who get the best grades learn the least. You can guess what happens to the ones least like their instructors. In such a novel environment they learn more, but their grades are rotten. You may have to think a while about this startling finding.

● **Biases.** When the same person who teaches you prepares and/or evaluates your test, watch out. His biases cannot help but influence the grading. With the best intentions, one is bound to think behavior like his own is good or right (and even charming).

● **Performance Criteria.** All the testing paraphernalia could be junked with no harm done. In real life, a simple "How are you coming along? does the trick. On the job, performance is self-evident.

---

[13]Unpublished research report by Dr. James Doerter, Southern Oregon College, Ashland, Oregon.

Staubach points out that a situation with artificial, contrived elements is a game and should be played as such. When you have lots of money riding on the outcome, as all students do, play to win.

FOUR GENERAL RULES

● **Business.** In a money game, don't get emotionally involved. This is business.

● **Sentiment.** Don't get sentimental about your opponent during a game.

● **Humor.** Develop a sense of humor. Concentrate on this and let your side vision take care of the details. Imagine you are the test maker planning your next move.

● **Expertise.** Become an expert on testing. Make up ridiculous tests as part of your study routine. You will be surprised how many of your ridiculous questions appear on the next test.

Think of tests as mind games.

Analysis of a Sample Test

You become an expert by learning to think like your opponent. Better still, use your opponent's strategies and his mistakes to your advantage. For a start, analyze the following test. First take it in your usual way. Then read our commentary.

TEST YOUR . . . WHAT?

Allow yourself a maximum of eight minutes. Then check your answers.

1. Allow yourself five minutes to rearrange the letters O-W-D—E-N-A-R-W to spell a new word—but not a proper name, nor anything foreign or "unnatural." Write it out.

2. Quickly now: How many animals of each species did Adam take aboard the Ark with him? (Note that the question is not how many *pairs* , but how many *animals*.)

3. What unusual characteristics do these six words have in common?
DEFT SIGHING CALMNESS CANOPY FIRST STUN
(Please complete your answer within five minutes.)

4. Figure out this problem in diplomatic relations: If an international airliner crashed *exactly on the U. S.-Canadian border, where would they be required by international law to bury* the survivors? (If you can't decide within *one minute* what your answer will be, please go on to the next item.)

5. What is the minimum number of active baseball players on the playing field during any part of an inning?

6. Figure out this problem within *one minute*: If one face of a cube measures 2″ x 4″, what is the area of *each* of the faces, and what is the *total* area of all eight faces? (Jot down your answer in the margin.)

7. A farmer had 17 sheep. All but nine died. How many did he have left?

8. An archeologist reported finding two gold coins dated 46 B. C. Later, at a dinner in his honor, he was thoroughly and openly discredited by a disgruntled fellow archeologist. Why?

9. A man living in Winston-Salem, North Carolina, may not be buried in a state west of the Mississippi River—nor in Hawaii or Alaska— even in the event of Presidential intervention. Why is this?

10. If you went to bed at 8 o'clock last night, and set your alarm clock to get up at 9 o'clock this morning, why on earth—after 13 hours' rest, especially!—are you so sleepy today?

11. If you had only one match, and entered a room to start up a kerosene lamp, an oil heater, and a wood-burning stove, which would you light first—and why?

12. Quickly, now: Divide 30 by ½ , and add 10. What is the answer?

13. If your doctor gave you three pills, and told you to take one every half hour, how long would it require for you to take all of them?

14. Two men played checkers. They played five games, and each man won three. How do you explain this?

15. Look at these phrases, for a moment, to get them firmly in mind:

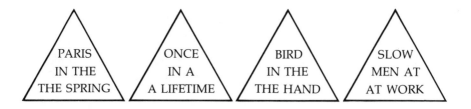

Now look away and write down these exact phrases.

Answers:

1. *a new word*, 2. It was Noah. 3. Each contains three letters in alphabetical sequence. 4. We do not bury survivors. 5. Ten. 6. It is not a cube. 7. Nine. 8. A coin printed before Christ was born would not have B.C. printed on it. 9. He is still alive. 10. The alarm would ring at 9:00 the same evening. 11. The match. 12. Seventy. 13. One hour. 14. They were not playing each other. 15. Notice the repetition of *the the, a a, the the,* and *at at.*

ITEM ANALYSIS

If you get one answer right on this test, you should score at least twelve. No matter how short the time allowed, always take some of it to look the whole thing over. In this case you would have discovered it is a trick test and logical reasoning is actually a hindrance.

1. You are allowed eight minutes for the total test. So naturally either you will save this one for last, or you will ignore the five minutes suggested.

In your preview of the test you see there are fifteen items. Allowing a minute to look over the test and a minute for review leaves six minutes for answering questions, a little less than half a minute each. Pace yourself and skip ones that seem hard until last. At some point you should catch on that the answers are right there on the page, but the test maker's game is to hide them from you. This is true of school tests, too.

The "correct" answer is *a new word.* The writer distracts you first by making it seem hard: "Allow yourself five minutes . . . ." Then, to take your eyes away from the phrase *a new word,* all sorts of useless instructions immediately follow. Your eye goes to them instead. Such instructions in most tests are intended to guide you. But here the test maker has used your reading strength against you. Once you catch on to a test maker's game plan, you can use it to your advantage. **Examine the motives of the test maker.**

2. It was *Noah.* Now we are on to his game. The "Quickly now" and the parentheses and underlining are all to keep you from noticing the word *Adam*. In this question and in the first question he does not use italics where they would have helped. He uses them only where they will distract you. Underhanded! Since it's the test maker's game, you can grumble, or you can turn his devices to your advantage. On any test, if you are familiar with the test maker's style, you can often spot the right answer. (More on this later.)

3. Thirteen of the questions on this test call for roughly the same *kind of thinking* and the same *level* of thinking. This question is different. It requires analysis that takes too long—unless you stumble on it accidentally. It is not really a trick. You have to change gears to discover the DEF, GHI, LMN, NOP, RST, and STU sequence. Every test has a few clinkers, and it is all right to miss them. Fiddle with them only if you have time left over.

Before you take a test, try to determine its level of difficulty so that you will know what level and kind of thinking the test maker accepts as "correct." Is it a game of old maid or bridge? Usually you will recognize a couple of questions, and these will cue your mind-set for that particular game.

4. Survivors are still *alive*. There he goes again. The test maker has used the same tricks three times now. We know his underlining and "helpful" additions are just dust in the eyes. So we strip the junk away and the real question stands out naked: Where are *survivors* buried?

In any test, read and think over the wording until you are sure what is really being asked. Nervous test takers often skim questions and misread them. **You cannot get emotional in a money game.**

5. *Ten.* There are too many right answers to this one. It was written poorly. Until we know what the test maker means by the word *active*, several answers work. If you are calm enough during a test, ask the test giver to define confusing words or instructions—before the test starts, if possible. You might otherwise be answering a question in *your* head but not in the test maker's. If the test giver won't help, give your best answer and write your reasoning in the margin.

6. A cube's sides are squares, and it has only six faces. In addition to the tricks we have already observed, the writer uses another habit against you. If you applied a math formula, you forgot this is a trick test. You don't have to know math for this test.

Again, as in number 5, you have to know what is really being asked. In problems such as this, *picture* the situation, even *draw* a picture to rough scale. Get the feel of the problem. Here, you would have discovered wrong information.

On a regular test, ask about errors you see, or write a note diplomatically telling why the question can't be answered. Test makers do make mistakes—aside from giving the test in the first place, that is.

7. Too easy. You already answered this in number 4. Use information and clues you find elsewhere in the test. A test contains plenty of facts. Use them to your advantage. The answer you need may be right there on the page in some other question or answer.

8. Picture the situation. Get the feel of the question. Come back later if it takes too long. B. C.!

9. Same as 2 and 4. Same tricks, too.

10. Visualize. Two and 6 call for the same process. You have to *see* what is happening.

Some test takers point out that there are twenty-four-hour clocks. But that fact is too sophisticated for this sort of test. Find the level of difficulty of the test and choose answers within that range.

11. Naturally a good reader thinks the word *which* refers only to *lamp*, *heater*, and *stove*. To trick you, the test maker counts on your reading the way most people would. But you know this is a trick test—and not very sophisticated either.

12. "Quickly, now . . . " is what throws you off. People get hurried and start in multiplying instead of dividing. **Put the question into your own words.** If you divide something by half, you are asking how many halves there are in it. In one there are two halves, right? So in thirty there are sixty halves.

13. Visualize. Picture the hands at, say, 7:00. You take your first pill at 7:00, your next at 7:30, your third at 8:00.

14. This is a rotten question. The test maker leaves out information you need in order to answer the question correctly. But knowing his other tricks, you could guess he is likely to do something like this. **Imagine you are the test maker planning your next move.** Information is sometimes left out in school tests, too.

15. Good readers read *ideas*, not words. Good habits trip you up here. Also the triangles camouflage the duplicated *the, a,* and *at*. Knowing the kind of test this is, though, and if you lucked out on number 11 and on number 14, you may be alert enough to *slow down* your normal response. **Visualizing and actually ticking off the parts helps.**

Review: Fifteen Test-Taking Tips

- **Examine any test before you start.**
  What kind of test?
  How hard?
  What level or kind of thinking?
  How many questions?

- Time yourself; assign a certain number of seconds per question. Stick to it.

- Allow time for review—*no matter what.*

- Save hard questions for last.

- See if the test maker tips his hand by his style, wording of questions or answers, or anywhere else.

- Ask for clarification on poorly worded questions.

- If necessary, amplify your answer in the margin.

- Some questions are clinkers. But answer all questions anyway.

- Read a question over until you are sure what it asks. Fight the temptation to skim.

- Review at the end to catch your clerical errors or to change answers you now know are wrong.

- Visualize or draw a picture. Jotting things down helps keep your thoughts steady and clear.

- A test contains hundreds of bits of information. Use them to deduce answers.

- Answer at the same level of sophistication as the test, not higher or lower.

- Ask about left-out necessary information, or write a note explaining why the question cannot be answered.

- Rephrase a tricky question until you see it in your own language.

All fifteen of these tips can be boiled down to the same three rules that were given for memorizing that appear in Chapter One:

Pay attention.
Rephrase.
Connect.

If you see the connection between the two activities, you won't have so much to remember. **Taking a test is simply retrieving**

stored data and using recall strategies that are a natural part of
your thinking.

How to Develop Test Awareness

Some people have no trouble reasoning their way through
life, but they get crumby test scores. It isn't that they are
stupid. It's simply that they have *a mind-set for failure*. They
seem to feel sure the game is hopeless, so they take tests *passively*. Tests feel alien. But once these same people catch on,
scores and grades go up. The process? First they get a good
look at test structure. They use item analysis to find out how
and where their thinking went wrong. Then, they practice
answering questions but in a specific way: by working their
way through *out loud* (or by writing down their thoughts as
they go). **Hearing or seeing what they are thinking makes
them conscious of their thought processes.** And that enables
them to reason their way through a problem *on purpose*. That is,
they learn how to learn. So you should

> **Analyze missed items,**
> and
> **Reason out loud.**

Once you make the processes **visible**, you will begin to use
them deliberately.

Psychologist Arthur Whimbey has coached people using
this approach and has seen marked changes in test results.[14]
Conscious analysis and deliberate reasoning are the key. Low
scorers frequently miss problems such as the following even
though all the problem really requires is following directions.

> *Cross out the letter after the letter in the word* seldom
> *which is in the same position in the word as it is in the
> alphabet.*

---

[14] Whimbey.

As Whimbey observes, some cross out the *d*. But that ignores the instruction to cross out the letter *after* the one that fits the requirement.

Actually, the question could easily have been worded more clearly. It is deliberately made difficult in order to test ability to wade through such stuff. (What does the word *which* refer to? This is like the trick question about the *lamp, heater,* and *stove*. Possibly this sort of skill would be good for bureaucrats.)

Instead of working on *seldom*, some crossed out the *d* in *word*. What went wrong? Probably they skimmed the question too quickly. A more patient reading or a couple of readings would have given the right answer. **To win, you have to hang in.**

By the way, the wording of a test question is often the worst part. Once you twist it into ordinary English, the problem itself is easy. For example, try to solve this problem. Then compare it with the rewording that follows.

> *I bought a car for $400 and sold it for $500. Then I bought it back again for $600 and sold it for $700. How much did I make in the used-car business?*
> *a. broke even, b. made $100, c. made $200, d. made $300*

Notice how much simpler it is when the wording is like this:

> *I bought a Plymouth for $400 and sold it for $500. Then I bought a Ford for $600 and sold it for $700. How much did I make in the used-car business?*

This example shows one reason we can say your score depends more on your being used to tests than on what you know. So don't feel too bad if you have had trouble. It takes patience to see what the real question is. Just fiddle with the wording until you *do* see what the test maker is driving at.

Thus, if wording is confusing, rephrase it until you see what the question actually is. Persist.

The instructions for some tests are so elaborate, especially some used for college and graduate-school entrance, that it really does take experience *beforehand* not to be overwhelmed. For example, from the College Entrance Examination Board Composition Test:

> *Here are sentences that are correct and acceptable. You are to give the sentence a new beginning. Then you must choose between phrases that would complete the new sentence, while keeping as close to the meaning of the original sentence as you can.*

10. Poetry, like all the other arts, is to a very large degree a mode of limitation.

    Begin with Poetry and all the other arts.

    (A) has to be (B) have to be (C) has always been (D) are (E) is

When you know you will be tested, get hold of a similar test and practice on it just to get used to the instructions and format.

Here, then, are some habits that out-loud analysis helps eliminate:

FIVE COMMON TEST-TAKING ERRORS

● **One-shot thinking** instead of a step-by-step path to the answer. Reason your way through. Expect to do well. Hang in.

● **Allowing gaps.** Expecting to fail, the reader allows his understanding to be fuzzy. So use the information given and persist until you have a clear picture.

● **Rushing through instructions.** Don't.

● **Skipping instructions.** Don't.

● **BEING PASSIVE.** This is the main barrier to high scores. Low scorers seem to think that the answer must be there right now or there is no way to reason it out. That is a mistake. After some success, low scorers see that they *can* work their way through lots of questions.

Six Tips for Good Scores

Do item analysis—out loud.

Get puzzle-question books and old tests.

Practice until you get good at it.

Get used to the format of tests you will have to take. Often the directions are the hardest part.

During study, practice making up your own questions.

Treat test taking as a game.

Item Analysis: Objective Tests

Try each question yourself. Then read the commentary. Reason your way through questions, but also watch for structural tip-offs.

MULTIPLE CHOICE

Example

Blah blah bah blah because

a. blah blah blah
b. blah bah blah
c. blah bah blah blah blah
d. blah blah bah blah

● **Longest answer.** The correct answer is c. Other clues failing, the longest answer is often the "right" one. The test maker worked harder on it. Most don't like to waste their talents and energy on wrong answers.

● **Explanation.** An involved explanation is often right, too.

● **Middle answer.** For want of other clues, take a stab at c. Test makers tend to put right answers in the middle. Better still, see if there is a pattern of length, location, or style for right answers.

Example

A general rule for memorizing is:

a. Memorize by rote in half-hour to one-hour sessions.
b. Put the material in your own words.
c. Repeat the material over and over.
d. Relax and let it steep.

● **Similar answers.** Similar answers may cancel each other out. Since a and c mean roughly the same thing, they are probably both wrong. That leaves only b and d. If they both seem right, pick the one that seems better. Here, b is correct.

Cross out wrong answers as you go. It is less confusing.

Example

School may be defined as a game because

a. time limits are set.
b. many people participate.
c. there is a leader.
d. it has artificial and arbitrary rules.

● **Most inclusive answer.** Choose d. The other answers may be true, but d is big enough to include them. So pick a broad answer instead of a specific fact or detail.

Example

The best time to review for a test is

a. immediately before you go to bed.
b. during a lunch break.
c. on weekends.
d. immediately after you get up.

● **Opposites.** Often, when opposites appear on a test, one of them is likely to be the answer. And b and c are not too likely. Common sense suggests they simply aren't inclusive enough. That cuts down the choices. Here, a is correct.

Example

Which of the following are forms of recall tests? a. Gallup and Robinson's Impact Post-Test, b. dummy magazine tests, c. portfolio tests, d. television recall tests.

1. a and d
2. a, c, and d
3. a, b, and c
4. a, b, c, and d

● **Process of elimination.** Looking over choices possible, you see a in all, and d has the word *recall* in it. So answer 3 is eliminated. That would still leave three possibilities, but we noticed earlier in this same test appears a true-false statement. In it is a phrase which suggests we can eliminate another answer:

> T F The great advantage of portfolio tests
> over *other forms of recall tests* is the
> fact that it closely duplicates
> normal exposure to an ad.

So c is apparently a form of recall test, too. That leaves b in doubt, narrowing the answer down to 2 or 4. Keep an eye peeled while taking the test; there might be another giveaway on what a dummy magazine test is. Without knowing much, you can narrow the question down to that one item: Is a dummy magazine test a recall test? And that could easily be the one thing you do know already about this test item. You can see that working out an answer as we have here is a lot like doing a cross-word puzzle. And it can be just as amusing.

By the way, a test format such as that above can bog down an inexperienced player. One technique is to go through marking answers T or F. Then see what you have left. And look the whole test over for further clues.

SUMMARY

Other things being equal, choose the longest answer or an involved explanation. Scan correct answers for a stylistic pattern: Usually the longest? Usually the shortest? Cross off similar answers. Choose a broad answer over specific or partial answers. Choose a middle-value answer, not an extreme. If two answers are opposites, one of them is likely to be the correct one. Scan for and cross out obviously wrong answers. For all- or none-of-the-above kinds of questions, mark each answer T or F as you go and then select. If all else fails, choose answer c. Look for help elsewhere in the test.

You don't really need to memorize all this. Just take time to understand the general idea now. When you are in a test situation, let your nerve endings guide you. Just keep the test in its proper place, that's all.

TRUE-FALSE

Example

T F It is not necessary to review your test answers.

● **Tricky wording.** Be careful marking your answer. By the time you convert the statement in your mind to "It *is* necessary . . . " you may have got the question turned around and might mark T by mistake.

● **Absolutes: False.** If a true-false statement contains **always, never, all, none, impossible,** and the like, it is likely to be a **false** statement. School people seem to despise absolutes. So, unless you are sure, mark it **false.** Exceptions will have been emphasized in class.

● **Tentative: True.** If there is a wishy washy word like **seldom, perhaps,** or **generally** the test maker is likely to want the answer **true.**

Note also the test maker wants you to agree with him, as in the question above.

Example

T F This statement is false.

The statement may be either true or false or both, so whichever way you answer, add a marginal comment explaining why.

Example

T F Persistence will result in higher test scores.

Here, the wording is ambiguous. You have to figure out what answer the test maker wanted. Does he mean *always?* Does he mean *persistence* alone? Does he mean *may* result? You may know perfectly well the role persistence plays, but that is not the problem. The problem is to figure out the test maker's mind.

Example

T F Persistence alone will result in higher test scores.

Answer it *false* because of the word *alone.* Even so, there is some room for argument. Maybe some experimenter varied only persistence and, sure enough, it alone turned the trick. So try to get on the same wave length as the test maker.

Example

T F It is not always necessary not to review.

● **Two negatives.** You do find pairs of negatives in tests. The difficulty is how to wade through the wording, not whether you know something. This sort of brain twister is practically impossible, so save it to play with later. Do choose some answer, though. Or write the answer in plain English in the margin.

If part of a true-false statement is wrong, the whole thing is wrong.

SUMMARY
Other things being equal, mark absolutes *false* **and tentatives** *true.* **Agree with the test maker. Save brain twisters for later. Review for mismarked answers. And use other questions and answers for clues.**

MATCHING

Work from one column and check off used-up answers as you go. Don't draw lines; they can make a confusing snarl if you have to change your answers.

SENTENCE COMPLETION

Example

Coaching can raise an
a. IQ score.
b. student's doubts.
c. tester's ire.
d. doubt of validity.

● **Grammatical tip-off.** The word *an* is a grammatical tip-off. You need a vowel sound after it. So the first answer, a, is the only one that fits. Read the stem with each answer to check for sentence tip-offs.

Sometimes a synonym gives it away and sometimes the verb.

Example

Test makers think aptitude tests measure

a. learning.
b. past experience.
c. knowledge.
d. talent.

Talent is a synonym for *aptitude*, so d is likely.

Example

Winning Through Intimidation is about

a. gaining wisdom through meditating.
b. showing power in order to overwhelm an opponent.
c. mutual-aid groups.
d. the Youth Conservation Corps.

The similarity of the idea in b to that of the title gives b away as the most likely answer.

COMPARISON

Example

The saying, *No rose but which has its thorns,* means most nearly:

a. The sweetest smelling rose has its perfume.
b. Touch not the thorn which grows on a rose.
c. No rare gem without its flaw.
d. Malice seldom wants a mark to aim at.
e. Where there is smoke there is fire.

Usually if there is one such question on a test, there will be several. The best defense is advance practice. If you come upon them cold, play with a few until you know you are onto the game. Then go back and work the first ones again.

Reasoning your way through is a knack acquired through experience, either then and there or earlier. The answer is not supposed to pop right out at you. You are expected to figure it out. Practice out loud is good preparation.

(Aside from the need for familiarity with the format, this question also penalizes inexperienced readers. The style of the phrase *but which* and the seldom-used meaning of the word *wants* may confuse students who are not used to them. So certain social backgrounds get the edge here. Stay as flexible as you can and try to allow the context to guide you to the most likely meaning of an expression.)

Reasoning through the problem above, first try to put it in your own words, possibly in more general terms:

> "Any valued thing has its drawback." *What relationship is emphasized?* [Valued thing plus negative aspect.] *In a,* perfume *is a positive aspect. Answer b contains a warning; the original statement does not. Answer c, of course, is correct. It has the same relationship as the original. Answer d involves elements external to the original relationship; nor is the relationship limited to valued things. Finally, e contains a negative aspect and a negative thing.*

Key: Practice and Persistence.

CRITICAL ANALYSIS

Example

Make a word from each of the following:

a. GMINHTAC
b. LURESTSAFE
c. CAIRNOSOMP
d. LIPLUMET

The answers are in this section: a. MATCHING, b. TRUE-FALSE, c. COMPARISON, d. MULTIPLE. Use the test itself as a field of information, for clues and for giveaways.

ANALOGY

Example

Select the pair of words which has a relationship most like that of the original pair.

TRIGGER:BULLET ::
a. handle : drawer
b. holster : gun
c. bulb : light
d. switch : current
e. pulley : rope

Such questions appear in aptitude and general-ability tests. But critics point out that such tests measure only previous experiences in working with such relationships and one's prior information. Such questions should be translated into regular English as follows: " *Trigger* has the same relationship to *bullet* as *what* to *what?*" Take some time first to see how *trigger* is related to *bullet*. The trigger *activates* the bullet. What relationship listed is just like that? The only one that works is d.

This is a simple example of an *analogy-test* item. It is supposed to test thinking ability. Libraries have sample tests and puzzle books for practice. As with most tests, there is a knack to them. You will improve your score if you get used to the format in advance.

Wouldn't it be nice if such "tests" were given and taken as recreational diversions rather than administered as valid indicators of intellectual and social worth?

How to Get High Scores on Essay Tests

To get good grades on essay tests, practice writing answers to questions you yourself make up. You will probably find the same or similar questions on the test. In class be sure of what is being asked before you start in, even if you have to read the directions several times. Inexperience and misunderstanding put you at a disadvantage.

Supposedly essay tests measure ability to organize, draw conclusions, relate ideas, and so on. In practice, they are most often simply recall tests, with the facts embedded in sentences instead of listed in phrases. The test giver probably has such a list and scores you on how many of the facts appear in your paper. Obviously a good player would memorize a similar list using a memory device (mnemonics) and jot it down somewhere before he even reads the test questions. Then he would see that they get stuffed into the paper somehow. Smooth connections from one to the other may help some, but your social science teacher doesn't have much time for checking your quality. He will skim for the key ideas (facts) and will not usually have time to enjoy original thinking either. Writing answers to essay questions is not as complicated as you may have been led to believe. It is a memory test, and you know good memory strategies already.

SIX GENERAL RULES FOR ESSAY TESTS

● **When you get the test, jot down your memory devices first,** before you read anything that might confuse you. That way, you won't build anxiety about forgetting.

● **Then read through the test,** noticing how much time is allowed, how many of the questions must be answered, which ones are easier, if there is credit for answering extra questions. Be sure you know what is expected and what will be credited.

● **Allot time for each answer and stick to this schedule.** If all questions are worth the same credit, give them equal time. In order to catch clerical and factual errors, leave some time at the end of the test to review your work.

● **Do easy questions first.** Answer exactly what is asked and stop. Save left-over time for playing with questions you think you could never answer. You could.

● **Not really knowing the answer to the question asked, some students will change the subject.** That irritates the test reader. You won't get much credit for a beautifully written wrong answer.

● **Get used to what is meant by common test directions.** (See below.)

Common Test Directions

Compare and contrast. "Compare *The Death of a Salesman* with *Our Town.*" How are they like each other? How are they different? Stuff in enough facts to make it stick. This type of instruction doesn't require your opinion.

Define. "Define *hollyfud.*" Just tell what it is. Give enough information so that it won't get mixed up with any other thing. Tell what is unique about it.

Discuss. "Discuss the four main causes of the Civil War." Put down what the teacher and text say are important about each one. Describe each one and tell how and why each helped to start the war. Test-analyst Staubach suggests describing it in terms understandable to the teacher *and* to a moron.

Criticize. "Criticize the Monroe Doctrine," Write about its quality, both its good and bad points. Stick to conventional views, unless you are sure the teacher wants *your* opinion. Judge it good/bad, true/false, right/wrong according to whatever view was supported in class by your teacher or is expressed in your text.

Be sure to read the directions carefully. "Criticize Shakespeare's *Hamlet*" is quite a different instruction from "Criticize the production of *Hamlet* performed here last Friday." In the first, as you can see, it is the play itself; in the second, it is the production. But, if you are nervous or in a hurry, you could misread the instruction. So deliberately slow down.

Trace. "Trace the development of American economic stability in California from the beginning until 1900." Put the events in a time sequence. First, on scratch paper, jot down dates and events in a column. Then in your paper put these facts into sentences and tie one into the next. Usually there will be three to five key items, with possibly a few minor facts tossed in.

Illustrate. "Two wrongs don't make a right. Illustrate." Tell a story it reminds you of. To put it another way, *illustrate* means to draw a picture. That can mean to draw a picture in words or to make a sketch or both.

Other words that crop up in essay tests: **describe, diagram, enumerate, explain, justify, list, outline, prove, review,** and **summarize.** You probably know what they mean. But don't get spooked and change the directions inside your head. If asked to **enumerate,** don't kibbitz and write an **evaluation** as well.

Twelve Grade-Raising Strategies

● **Check over your essay.** Wherever you repeat a noun, replace it with another word that means the same thing. Or stuff in a fact. It makes your work look more knowledgeable. Wherever you can, use nouns instead of pronouns. If you've forgotten what a pronoun looks like, here is a list:

I	they	them	its	hers
we	who	whom	their	theirs
you	me	my	whose	
he	us	our	mine	
she	him	your	ours	
it	her	his	yours	

● **Use lots of paragraphs.** It makes a paper look organized. Insert roughly one new fact in each. This makes it easier for the test reader to skim for the facts on his list.

● **Write as neatly as you can.** Research shows it can get you as much as a grade higher than the same words sloppily written.

● **Leave lots of space between answers for later additions.**

● **In blue-book tests, leave the left-hand page blank.** If you think of something to add, write it there, and draw a neat arrow to the spot where it belongs. Even at the cost of neatness, *do* cross out or correct errors.

● **If only four questions will be credited, don't waste time doing five.**

● **Do answer every question that will be credited.** Write *something*. You can't get credit for a blank page. (More on credit for knowing nothing later.)

● **Write as though you were explaining something to a kid in the seventh grade, directly and simply. Pretend you are having a conversation.** What questions would a seventh grader have? Answer them.

● **Don't criticize a test question in your essay answer, unless you don't care about your grade.** Make the best of a bad situation.

● **Avoid being folksy, cute, or apologetic. Just say it and stop.** Some teachers don't care for "I think . . . it seems to me . . . in my opinion . . . " and the like, either. So avoid them.

● **Leave time to review and proofread.**

● **If you run out of time for your last answer, put in an outline or list your facts in a column.** You may get almost full credit, depending on the test reader and *his* list of facts. Give it a try. Next time, pace yourself.

Hanging-in Tactics

● **Mental block.** If it really is a mental block, deliberate retrieval strategies should get things flowing again. Get something on that blank sheet of paper. You are almost sure of getting *some* points. This is a Where-were-you-on-Valentine's-Day-three-years-ago situation. You know something about all sorts of things, and when you start tracing them back, you will find them all connected. So let's get to work.

A good way to come unstuck is just to start writing—anything remotely connected to the subject. "What were the four causes of the Civil War?" Write anything at all. As you write you will begin to remember things. Your brain is a connecting organ. One thing leads to another, and all are interconnected. Use your retrieval strategies, but be sure to put down the thoughts as they come so that you will have some words on paper. What you need is in there. It just needs to be teased out. You do know some things about the Civil War: Lincoln, his assasination, slavery, cotton, the Grey and the Blue, England and France, Sumpter,   Peachtree Street.   The Mason-Dixon line, John Brown, Carl Sandburg, Rhett Butler, Northern factories, transportation, Gettysburg, Lee, *Huckleberry Finn*.

Then step back and see what you have done. By this time you may be able to see an overall pattern. If you do, you can go back and insert or cross out. Insert topic sentences and connecting sentences. Write a summary. Someone skimming for facts will not pay too much attention to your style. You have more information than you guessed, and your paper will probably read much better than you thought possible.

To take this approach, you have to like yourself enough to want to give it a try. You are as good as everyone else in the room. You have a right to top grades. You wouldn't give up in basketball; don't give up in this game either.

●   **Unprepared.** If you really didn't study, the day of the test is no time to panic. You are there; it *is* a game; see what you can salvage. **Never give up in a school game.** Keep in mind that some of those papers that will get the top scores are written by bull artists. In a game like that, you have a right to hang in there until they drag you out. Only a born masochist would leave the page blank. You would have to have total cultural amnesia to be that empty.

Suppose you are to identify Franklin Roosevelt, for example. The reader will be looking for facts. Maybe you get five points for the question. Okay, let's dig up and stuff in some facts:

> Franklin Roosevelt was a *Twentieth Century President* who had a strong *influence on American life,* despite the *crippling paralysis* [You saw two minutes of *Sunrise at Campobello* on TV once] that confined him to a wheelchair. His wife *Eleanor* became famous herself. He was the *second Roosevelt in the White House.*

It's not much, but you may pick up some credit, and that may be just enough to save your skin. **Always try.**

SIX COMMON QUESTIONS ON TAKING TESTS

● **The best attitude?** It is good to be a little but not too anxious. If you are too smug, you will be careless with easy questions, too tense and you keep trying the wrong strategy (tunnel vision). Psychologist W. Lambert Gardiner puts it this way: **Sweat if it's easy; relax if it's hard.** Don't assume you will fail; don't be nonchalant. Get every point you can.

● **Cramming?** If you haven't paced your work earlier, sure, take every break you can get. But plan your attack. Don't just wade in and try to read everything you put off all these weeks. Get an overview of the stuff. Find the general outline and main points. Follow the steps of routine review given below.

● **Lack of sleep?** You can get along without sleep well beyond twenty-four hours. If you have your wits about you and can remain cool, conceivably you could sit up all night preparing. Psychologically, however, people often get more anxious the longer they spend going over material. In general, the best strategy is to get a good night's sleep.

● **Take the night off before a test?** No. Living it up before a test doesn't really work—at least there's no research to support it. There is plenty to suggest you should put in a reasonable amount of study and go to bed. A couple of hours of review are plenty. Sleep reinforces and fixes what has been studied (like Jell-O), provided nothing else has gone on in between.

● **Review?** If you have made useful notes right in your text (more on this in Chapters Three and Four), review these. Your own markings will provide the gist of the chapter. What are the author's main points? There will be three to five or so per chapter. How does the writer support them? Once you have retrieved this overview from your earlier study, make up questions like those you think will be on the test. Brush up on any weak areas.

Use this very same technique for cramming: Outline the chapters, but don't try to read the material. Count on your test-taking skills to pull you through.

● **Extra study?** A little overlearning is good, but excessive study can wreck your nervous system. Deliberately plan a length of time for review, proceed systematically, and stop.

GAME PLAN FOR TAKING TESTS

Before the Test: Five Tips

● **The night before, review two to three hours just before bed time.** If you have studied efficiently earlier, you may not need this much time.

● **Get up at a normal time for you.** Treat the day as routinely as possible. But do allow enough time for a nourishing breakfast (unless you hate breakfast, in which case stick to your regular habits). A high-protein breakfast helps keep blood sugar up all day and keeps on providing necessary energy. A shower and some light exercise may help.

● **A few minutes leafing through your review materials will reinforce memory of key ideas.**

● **Arrive at class early enough to get seated and lay out necessary materials.** Getting there too early or too late increases tension. Talking with friends may shake your confidence too.

● **Sit where you are most comfortable, probably your usual seat.** But avoid sitting with a friend. Distractions of any sort should be avoided.

During the Test: Thirteen Tips

● **Before you even look at the test, jot down on the back memory devices and facts you are afraid of forgetting.**

● **Examine the whole test quickly before you start in.** Make sure you understand the general instructions. If there is more than one way to interpret them, ask the instructor which meaning he intends. Ask about test items that aren't clear to you, too.

● **Notice time limits and figure out how much time you should allow for each question. Leave a couple of minutes to review.**

● **Remember, go through once, building your confidence with easy questions first.** Remember, also, that you can find answers in other questions or can eliminate wrong answers because of wording or logical inconsistencies. Play with hard questions.

● **If you start to get tense, come back later.** Do some muscle tensing and relaxing exercises. Or breathe slowly and deeply counting your breaths for one minute.

● **Never leave blanks even if there are penalties for guessing.** People who do guess get better scores than those who don't.

● **Read over questions two or three times if necessary until you are sure you know what is being asked.** Watch out that you don't misread the question and answer some question in your own head instead of the one on the test.

● **First answers are not always best.** Studies show that people who change answers score higher generally on the changed answers.

● **Unless you have reason to do otherwise, treat questions as though they are being asked honestly.** But do think like the test maker.

● **People often pick up extra points when they check their work.** So allow time for this.

● **If you are asked to choose the *best* answer, even if they are all bad, pick the best one.**

● **In math solve the problem *before* you look at the multiple choice answers.** Otherwise, you may tend to work the problem to fit one of the answers.

● **Don't quit until they blow the whistle.** Persist. Let the others leave. Squeeze out every point you can.

After the Test: Where the Real Game Begins

● **As soon as your test is returned to you, do an item analysis.** Knowing what went wrong can build you into a master test taker. How was your game off? What techniques will prevent you from getting caught again? A good player considers his failures to be *information* he can use. In a money game, don't get emotional.

● **Analyze the first quiz in any class for clues or giveaways**

in the test maker's style or format. You can figure out the level and kind of thinking wanted by seeing what answers were considered "right." Which of your strategies worked well or poorly on this quiz? What kind of questions should you make up for practice next time?

● **After the first quiz, no matter how well you did, ask for an appointment to go over your wrong answers with the teacher:** "There are a couple of items I'd like to talk about." Don't say the whole test was a complete mystery. Faculty egos are vulnerable.

The purpose of your visit, in reality, is to make the teacher conscious of your existence and your "interest" in the course. He will remember your scholarly attitude. If there is a coin toss to decide your C or B grade, you want the psychological weight in your favor. The idea is for the teacher to feel that if you fail he has failed, too. After all, he worked with you regularly throughout the course.

● **If you fail a test, stay confident.** Remember a test rarely measures what you really know nor does it show how smart you are. No grade is final. There is always something more you can do. School is a game and there are lots of ways to score. Item analysis should reveal what tack is appropriate. Then go for it: A make-up test, an extra project, a better game plan for future tests, a conference with the teacher (let him suggest something), a tutor, a different study approach, transfer to a different teacher, an extenuating-circumstances grade change, withdrawal from the course. Get the idea? But keep your solution in line with the problem. A popgun may be all that is needed.

● **Take your score with good humor.** It is only one inning. Even if this particular game is over, there is a rematch just up ahead. And you will be ready.

SUMMARY

Most people are too anxious during tests. Their concern clouds their reasoning and makes them less efficient than normal. Off balance, they score far lower than they should. No one who is going to spend twelve to sixteen years or more taking tests should endure this unnecessary handicap.

The solution, of course, is to learn the rules and techniques of successful test taking. Success builds assurance, which in turn frees us to perform better and better. Once one realizes that eight-tenths of his score depends on *how* he takes a test, it becomes obvious that learning rules of the test-taking game is crucial. It is not complicated. One does not have to be clever, brilliant, or dishonest to do it. It is a matter of observation and practice.

Oddly, most people have not really thought much about what it means to make, give, and take tests. Once they see tests are school games that have little actual meaning in the real world, once they realize the game has a format that can be recognized, rules that can be mastered, playing strategies that can be learned, it can become as entertaining as Scrabble or crossword puzzles.

Mastering test taking, like learning to absorb and retrieve information, is part of the process of educating oneself. So the effort will not be wasted or pointless. Figuring out tests is a problem-solving experience. And developing confidence to recognize and solve problems is not just a school game but a true educational activity.

3

Reading Textbooks

IN THIS CHAPTER

SYNOPSIS

Reading time can be reduced by two-thirds by approaching an assignment as a problem in information processing. The trick is to identify and overcome barriers to understanding, either in the print or in one's own reading habits. Any ordinary reader is equipped to do this.

The chapter begins with the advice to plan a little in advance and follow through afterward with some review and reinforcement (as was suggested for memorizing and for taking tests). The approach is compared with that for any problem. First, four sample strategies and eight problem-solving questions lead up to typical problems experienced with printed matter (too hard, too complicated, style unfamiliar, too easy, too boring) and some practical solutions. These boil down to consciousness of alternatives and persistence.

Next four samples for practice from college reading precede transcriptions for comparison condensed from the attempts of other college students.

The foregoing ideas and suggestions are compressed into a four-part study-reading method of general usefulness: BFAR (Browse, Focus, Absorb, Reinforce). The BFAR method is the central idea of the chapter and should be read carefully. (It will also be used for listening to lectures, Chapter Four). The process includes a system for marking key ideas and for keeping notes in the text margins. Rephrasing is suggested to help keep the new material in mind. In addition, a method for mapping the structure of a chapter or a section is described.

The chapter then lists ten reader errors and recommends remedies.

A nutshell speed-reading course appears on page 113 along with an instant vocabulary course on page 114.

The summary reminds you that reading is problem solving, and the BFAR approach is the same method you have probably already used successfully in out-of-school experiences.

THE TROUBLE WITH TEXTBOOKS

Textbooks that Cause Reading Problems

Reading takes up more of a student's time than any other school chore. Anyone who reads word-for-word everything assigned is spending two to three times too long on it—or more. It is not the only way to learn; it is not even the main way. The picture of reality each of us carries in his head is not a result of scanning print. It is infinite particles of information processed inside one's own self, organized, restructured, integrated, according to an inner scheme. That you learn only in school or from books is pure fiction. This life-long learning process goes on twenty-four hours a day. And we ourselves control what we learn through our background, our desire or need, and our habits. Wasting time on school books numbs the mind and the senses and thus retards education.

Stimulating and Stupefying Prose

Some ideas set in print are as stimulating as anything life can offer. One printed sentence can engage the mind for an hour or for days or a lifetime and be worth every second. Rare textbooks are like that. Most, as you know, are not. Some take hundreds of words to make an obvious point, ignore real difficulties, and are so monotonous that no one wants to read them. People who can read self-selected books brilliantly are often "stupid" when it comes to texts. No wonder; such writing can stupefy. But there are ways around this drudgery. Sometimes it is not necessary to read the worst stuff at all.

A GENERAL APPROACH

The same techniques work for reading as are used for solving problems of any sort: Taking tests, fixing a motor, backpacking, retrieving information stored in one's mind. One approaches the work of a genius or a petty civil servant in the same way except that he may dwell happily at length on a sentence of the genius and scarcely pause over whole paragraphs or chapters of the other. In either case nothing is to be gained from spending one extra second on the reading itself.

An alert learner, reading some new article, will realize that there is a special set of words (only a few usually) or a special meaning of familiar words and some simple relationship holding those key words together. The job is to identify these words and this pattern.

Reading a textbook involves problem-solving procedures. Imagine the steps in getting ready for, taking, and remembering your first backpacking trip and you have the general approach:

Getting the feel of the problem
Making your plan
Trying it out
Reviewing your results

● **To read a textbook efficiently, plan a little in advance and follow through afterward with some review and reinforcement.**

Just plunging in and reading straight through is the worst approach and also the most common. When a task is self-chosen, people simply don't behave like that. But most students who have trouble with texts do. Reading from beginning to end without a plan takes too long and yields crumby understanding. Passive reading is boring. As Chapter One points out, purposeful strategy is needed. Following are four sample strategies, including eight questions you can ask yourself when you get stuck. Then come some typical problems and solutions.

Four Reading Strategies

READ BACKWARDS

Reading backwards is more productive than just starting in at the front! Of course, anything would be. If you try starting at the back, you will see it is not all that crazy. The gist is often bunched in a summary, and if that isn't clear you browse backwards until it is. Possibly less than halfway to the front, the idea will make sense and you can quit reading.

The backwards technique simply forces you to pay attention, put it in your own words, and connect it with what you already know. It requires active processing of information. The point is, if you have *some* system, it will work much better than if you don't. And not being dominated by the textbook's authority gives you the confidence to use your own brain. You are in this for yourself, not for your teacher nor for the textbook writer. You are free to get meaning any way you can dream up.

READ THE BOLD PRINT AND LOOK AT PICTURES.

If you keep your wits about you, this might work. Certain books don't deserve more. If that is the case, this much preparation may be all you need. Just go through reading the bold print and looking at the pictures.

This approach will give you the pattern of the chapter and the author's main points. You may have enough background that you can supply your own supporting evidence. And the ideas may be simple enough that no explanation is necessary. This overview gives you the way ideas are structured and shows their relation to each other. As you know from Chapter One, you have to find the pattern anyway in order to commit the new stuff to memory.

While you are browsing and skimming you also get a chance to see how the ideas can be fitted in with what you already know. Once you see the overall pattern, if any parts are fuzzy you can come back and examine them more carefully. You may want to read a paragraph here and there and think about it a while. But let your needs determine that.

FIGURE OUT THE ASSIGNMENT

If the assignment itself is fuzzy, you could waste hours doing too much work or the wrong kind. The first problem may be to figure out what the teacher really wants when he says, "Read Chapter Two." It could be any of these:

Get the general idea of it.
Be able to give the main idea and its supporting details.
Give the main idea in your own words and supply your own examples.
Thoroughly memorize the main and supporting ideas word for word.

Or whatever. Clear that up first. It may be possible the teacher will cover the very same material in class and the general outline is all you need.

DEVISE A PLAN

When you hit a snag, figure a way through or around it. The material may contain some problem that browsing and skimming can't solve. You will need to come up with a plan of some sort. Keep in mind that any difficulty can be overcome. In fact, **there are always many alternatives. Make that your cardinal rule.** Once you take a look at a chapter, you will have to figure out what is in the way and remove it. The problem could be almost anything. If you are falling asleep, you could stand up to read, read twice as fast, read backwards, or force attention by moving your hand along the page as a pacer. If the text is impossibly difficult, you could always get someone else to read it and explain it to you or work through it with you. Just be alert to stumbling blocks and use your imagination.

How do you identify the stumbling blocks? Just ask, "What's stopping me here?" Is it the whole chapter, just a few passages, or some concept? Is it the style: too commonplace to keep you curious, too pretentious, too distant from your experience, the layout? Some readers will close a book just because they don't like the look of the print style. If you can identify what is really causing the trouble, the solution is close. Solve it just like any other problem:

EIGHT PROBLEM-SOLVING QUESTIONS

● **Have I had the same problem before or one somewhat like it?** (Not necessarily in reading: A situation like fixing an electric motor or a problem in carpentry or in tennis might suggest what to do next.) **Would a solution like that work here?**

● **How did I solve some other problem? Would something like that work here?**

● **Can I turn the problem upside down or say it or see it a different way?**

● **Can I work on other parts of it?** If so, gradually work back to the difficulty.

● **Can I at least solve just part of it?** There is usually something familiar to start on.

● **Can I say it more narrowly? More broadly?** Something

helpful might show up.

● **What things do I already know that could help me here** (from any field, not just reading)?

● **How can I state the problem in different words? Are there now possibilities I didn't see before?**

Using such questioning as the above, decide on a plan. Then try it out. If you succeed, reread the passage and see if it is clear now.

In print, following such a questioning process may seem too time consuming, but actually it can be accomplished in a flash, in just a couple of seconds. It is just a matter of getting clear, *grokking*, as Heinlein would put it.

Some Typical Reading Problems and Possible Solutions

TOO HARD

Narrow it down. Is the problem vocabulary, style, complexity, lack of experience with the subject?

Vocabulary Unfamiliar.

If it is just a few words (skimming and browsing will reveal this) they are usually explained as you read along. Don't dwell on individual words at first. Just get the general idea. If the words actually prevent understanding, look them up—but only after you have read through the passage at least once.

Too Many New Words

Don't try to master them all. As above, get an overview from the pictures and bold print. When necessary, see if you can break the word into its parts, the roots and affixes. Words from Latin and Greek so often found in school books use the same parts over and over, and you probably already know many of these. Many can be translated into ordinary English.

● **Read a different, clearer writer on the same subject.** Often the unfamiliar words are just the author's style, not the subject you are studying. Pick some other writer you can understand. New subjects are hard enough without having to figure out the author, too.

● **Use the index as a word list.** There is no quicker way to discover what the author thinks is important. The more space the word takes up, the more important it is. How often does it crop up; how many page numbers are listed? How many of the words in the index are unfamiliar?

● **Relax about vocabulary.** Drudges list and look up every new word in a chapter. It is unnecessary and somewhat insane. Instead, work for understanding, and study vocabulary only when absolutely necessary (or when you have nothing else to do). Students don't have time to look up every new word. You will learn thousands and thousands while in college without this agony. As you learn new ideas, the words follow.

Ideas too Strange

Chemistry? Astronomy?

● **Make it familiar.** Compare it with something you do know. Usually it is not the whole thing but just some aspect causing the trouble. *What is it like?* Soft ball? Fishing? Reading music? How did you master that? Try a similar approach, or see it the same way.

● **Try a kids' book.** You can find beautifully written books for kids covering almost any college subject. They are clear and use simple, direct language. Some college text writers could take lessons from them. Get the general idea from the kids' book and then fill in the necessary details from your text. If you are proud, tell the children's librarian it is for your little brother.

● **Classic comics work, too.**

● **Explain it to someone else, even to the TV.** Or at least put it in your own words. Snags often break loose this way.

TOO COMPLICATED

● **Browse until you find something you can grasp.** Then work backwards and forwards filling in the picture with more and more details until the idea makes sense.

● **Talk it out.** Discuss it with someone else, a friend, a tutor in the study lab, your teacher.

● **A table of contents shows the book's structure.** You can find relationships there. You can see what is considered more important and what less. You may have let yourself get bogged down on an unimportant point. Check the table of contents to rule this out.

● **Work a problem or read examples first.** Often an explanation or directions will make more sense to you if you work backwards. You will have something to hang on to.

● **Draw a diagram or a picture as you go.** That will help keep things straight.

STYLE UNFAMILIAR.

Old fashioned sentence structure? Strange dialect? Unusual or complicated phrasing?

● **Start with the familiar.** Find something in the paragraph that makes sense and work in both directions from there.

● **Rearrange the sentence.** Move phrases around or leave them out temporarily until the sentence is simple and direct. That often solves the problem. Play with a messy sentence until it comes out in your own language. Then reread and see if it is now clear.

● **Compare it with things you do know.**

● **Try a hunch.** *Maybe it's like* . . . .

● **Try a different author or translation.** Translators can make Aristotle dreary or stimulating. Writers can kill physics or make it beautiful. Pick a style you like.

● **Try a movie or video tape on the author or the subject.** Your AV library may have just what you need.

● **Read the critics first.** Magazine articles on your book, your subject, your author, often clear things up. Those black holes in space, for example. *Time* had a cover story on them some time back. It explained the idea so that ordinary people could understand it. Or try short critical articles in encyclopedias. Go to the section in the stacks on your subject and browse the books there. *Popular Science, Popular Mechanics, Psychology Today, Time, National Geographic, Scientific American* often contain readable versions.

TOO EASY, TOO BORING.

Uninteresting stuff is hard to read. Do anything to avert boredom.

● **Browse, skip, skim.** Shoot for the **framework** and **key ideas**. You can see then if you need to read some of the explanations or examples. If one is enough, don't read six.

● **Check table of contents and index for organization and vocabulary.** You may not need to read further. Or you can narrow down your work.

● **Read backwards.** Social science and psychology texts tend to save the punch line for the last. So start there. Then, if you want to read all about the conditions of the experiment, you will know where it all leads. Or you may be able to skip the preliminaries.

● **Read a book that is better written.** A lousy, repetitious style can kill a subject. Shop around.

● **Read twice as fast** to force concentration.

● **Take frequent breaks.** Plan in advance how much you can bear in one session. Time yourself.

● **Turn it upside down.** Make it unfamiliar. *How can I stretch this boring thing out of shape so that I can regain interest in it.?* What else is this technical subject like? Converting Latinized explanations into ordinary language can do the trick. In *The Games People Play* Eric Berne points out that clients soon made up their own expressions to replace technical terms: *wooden leg, rapo, now-I've-got-you-you-son-of-a-bitch, look what you made me do,* and so on. Convert dry reading into something more juicy.

In General, Have Lots of Alternatives.

No two writers are the same. You will have to combine or vary your approach as you encounter new snags. But there will always be some way to get through or around them. **Be conscious of your successful tries, and use some version of them for similar problems.** Gradually you will develop dozens of tactics and will be able to use them automatically.

Getting what you want or need from print is not so much a matter of brilliance as it is one of having lots of alternatives. When we are passive, things seem difficult and we can build a habit of helplessness—even though we are perfectly capable of doing something. This defeatism develops apparently from being assigned things we don't care to do. School assignments often encourage this unsuccessful behavior. But from your own experience you know that when there is a strong need or desire, ordinary readers can understand complex, difficult material. A few successful experiences can generate the confidence that makes us persist long enough for the payoff.

Review and Reinforce

As you know, without deliberate storing and filing, memory fades. It is one thing to liberate ideas from print and quite another to hang on to them. Since new ideas fade so fast, it would be masochistic to stop before getting them into your memory bank. You don't want to have to do the work over again.

So once you find what you want, use memory techniques to fix it in mind. Notice the structure and create logical subgroups.

Test yourself.
Use flash cards.
Overlearn.
Make an analogy (comparison).
Persist.
Practice.

Always reinforce and then give yourself a little break. More on this most important step, **reinforcing,** in the section on study-reading (pages 104-105).

Samples for Practice

Whatever is on the printed page, or on someone's lips for that matter, it won't be the same by the time you process it inside your head. Ideas can't be transferred whole. They have to be chewed and digested, just as grass is redistributed as flesh, bones, and milk in cows. When you absorb a new idea, neither you nor it will ever be the same. That is why we say reading is thinking. Decoding the print itself is just the start. Then education begins. The process is natural, so with a little conscious practice you will catch on and will develop the knack.

Most people are not very flexible when they read. If they don't understand the first time through, they throw up their hands and quit. **But the only thing you can understand the first time through is something you already know.** New ideas take a quick read-through, a more careful reading, and usually a third checkup run through. All of that can be accomplished in less time than in one typical passive reading. Relax a bit and play with a passage, maybe put it in your own words. There are all kinds of approaches. Allow yourself a little time to succeed. You will get faster and faster as you gain experience. Following are a few samples to practice on.

WHAT TO DO.

These samples were taken from various kinds of college reading assignments. Do what you can on your own. After each of the first three samples is a transcription of the out-loud thinking of some students as they thought their way through the same passage. These are not word-for-word transcriptions, but they follow the general thought pattern. Naturally, there are many other approaches depending on background and ingenuity, some longer, some much shorter. You can compare your technique and see if any new possibilities emerge. If the passage is easy for you to understand, skip the transcription.

Sample One

Find the author's point. In other words, where *does* he live?

Where I Live

"Where do you live?" he asked. With a sudden shock I realized that this was a problem I had been confusedly thinking about for years. "Where do you live?" I handed him a card. But, needless to say, my address was not the answer to the riddle. . . .
It wasn't a question of streets or cities, not even of countries or continents; it was a question of universes. . . .
For what we are, what we know or think we know we are, determines where we live. Home, in a word, is homemade.

Out of the raw material of given experience each of us con-
structs his own particular universe. . . .

For the great majority of animals, the most conspicuous fea-
tures of every human universe are simply not there. Sun,
moon and stars, the sea and the dry land, all the wealth of
vegetation and the countless things that swim, crawl, fly and
run—the worlds, in which all but a very few species live, contain nothing that remotely resembles such objects. . . .

The nature of any island universe depends on the nature of
the individual inhabiting it. . . .

All human worlds are more brightly colored than those in-
habited by dogs. But not so deliciously smelly. All human
worlds contain much greater extensions of space than does the
world of the bees. To make up for this, the bees' world contains things which exist in no human world, such as two
kinds of light, polarized and unpolarized, and objects whose
color is ultraviolet. . . .

> Aldous Huxley, from "Where I Live," first published in *Esquire*.

TRANSCRIPTION OF AN APPROACH

*Let's see. Six short paragraphs. It will likely take less
than a minute to read, probably less than five or six to master. Browsing, I see the words and sentence style are no
problem. Browsing, I see from paragraph two he's not talking about addresses. Okay, what? Oh, I see this is an excerpt from a longer article. Starts in the middle. Browsing
still, I see references to other animals and separate universes.
I'm beginning to get the idea that he plans to change or
extend what is meant by* where one lives. *Okay. So it's a
new definition, then. I'll zip through now and see what he
means. Okay. The first two paragraphs tell what he* doesn't
*mean. He doesn't mean physical location on the earth.
What, then?*

*Oh, here it is in paragraph three. Where we live (he's
not just talking about himself but everyone) is where our
consciousness says we do. We build "where we live" from
our biological bodies and from our experiences.*

That's not too clear. Oh, here in paragraph four he gives some examples. Humans, he says, by our physical nature, are able to experience different worlds, even though we might be in the same spot. It's starting to be clearer. I wish he would give me something more definite. Okay, in the last paragraph he gives examples from dogs and bees, things humans experience and they can't, and vice versa.

All right, I think I have it now. I'll see if I can put it in my own words:

In the broader sense, my feeling of "home" (or my world) is determined by what my body and mind are able to sense and organize. All species have different sensors, so all have different "worlds" or "homes." In fact, even in the same species no two individuals can experience the same "home."

Can I supply an example of my own? Well, a bird must experience an airiness I could never grasp, but a bird can't imagine what riding a bicycle is like (big deal). Each student in a class has an entirely different data bank (home) from every other one.

Now I'll go back and underline something that will serve as the gist for review. Okay, I underline It's a question of universes *and the dog example. That should be plenty to trigger recall later.*

I'll read through again quickly and see if it's really clear now. It is.

Notice the reader has one problem to begin with: to get the author's point. But he redefines it as he gets familiar with the passage: to find a new meaning of "where I live." Then he reads fast for that one thing. When he thinks he has it, he puts it in his own words, marks the key idea, and then verifies it by a quick rereading. In print this process takes about 450 words, but people don't think in complete sentences. The reading and analysis could easily be done in a minute or two.

Hey, rereading, I got to thinking, "Why did he write this in the first place?" I think his real purpose was to celebrate or rejoice in the fact of unique worlds, the wonder of each creature being so different. He wants to share his enthusiasm about these universes. Since I "got the message," my island universe has a new dimension.

Notice that this reader goes a step further and wonders, So What? Most school assignments don't require this step. But in truth it is only at this stage that education begins. It is the part that is fun: Getting the feel of other worlds and expanding or enriching one's own.

Sample Two

Find Aristotle's main idea. Right away you will see it is a problem of style. See if you can get it into your own language. When you get it figured out, compare your approach with the transcript.

We must be content, then, in speaking of such subjects and with such premises to indicate the truth roughly and in outline, and in speaking about things which are only for the most part true and with premises of the same kind to reach conclusions which are no better. In this spirit, therefore, should each type of statement be received; for it is the mark of an educated man to look for precision in each class of things just so far as the nature of the subject admits; it is evidently equally foolish to accept probable reasoning from a mathematician and to demand from a rhetorician scientific proofs.

Aristotle

TRANSCRIPTION

Browsing, I see it's very short. What are premises? What's a rhetorician? Maybe I don't need to know or I can figure it out from the passage. Browsing, I can see sentence style is my main problem. If it were in my own way of say-

ing things I might be able to understand it. It's so short I think I'll read through it quickly.

That didn't help much. For one thing the first sentence is awfully long and it's general. There aren't any images for me to hang on to. Okay, I'll skip it for a moment. It looks like the second sentence is just another way of saying the first. All right, here at the end is a reference to mathematicians. I'll work on that. At least it's concrete. Cutting out extra words, he says, "It is . . . foolish to accept probable reasoning from a mathematician." All right, that I grasp. We expect him to be precise and exact. No guessing. Okay. He also says it's just as foolish, "equally" foolish, to expect a rhetorician to give scientific proofs. Swell. What's a rhetorician? I guess I'll have to deduce that to figure this thing out.

Probably he's something like the opposite of a mathematician, someone who doesn't pretend to deal in exact, precise, provable things. Maybe like a philosopher. Oh, I remember, rhetoric. I ran into that in English. Something to do with style, giving speeches. Ah: What you do to persuade people. You expect him to get at the feel of an idea, not the precise proof of it. Now back to the sentence.

We should expect precise stuff from the mathematician and we should expect probable stuff from the speech maker. Okay. Now let's see what the rest of the sentence says. ". . . look for precision . . . just so far as the nature of the subject admits [allows]" If it's poetry, expect one kind of thinking; if it's statistics, expect another kind. Don't mix them. So an educated person won't expect more or less than the nature of the thing calls for.

Now let's go back up to the first sentence. I see now that this is an excerpt and can only guess what the first part of the sentence refers to. What's a premise? Must be what comes before you get a conclusion, probably something like assumptions or arguments. Looks like the second half is another way of saying the first half. So, if something is mostly true, it doesn't mean it's always true. What's an example? Well, if I'm exposed to typhoid, you have to say

I'll probably *get sick. Now let's see if I can put it in my own words:*

For certain subjects I can only make general comments. I shouldn't draw more from the evidence than is justified. (I may not know enough.) Everything one hears should be checked in this manner. Educated people expect only as much precision as the original conditions make possible. It's foolish to expect a math teacher to talk like the speech teacher, and vice versa.

You go through the above thinking very quickly and may not need all the steps. For most readers the idea itself isn't hard. Getting used to the style is. But after some experience with it, it is rather charming. Take your time. Fool around with it. Grab something and work out from there. When the whole thing seems meaningless, get meaning from some simplified smaller whole. Then move to the more complicated whole.

Sample Three

What is the author's main point?

The only subject presented to me for study is the content of my consciousness. You are able to communicate to me part of the content of your consciousness which thereby becomes accessible in my own. For reasons which are generally admitted, though I should not like to have to prove that they are conclusive, I grant your consciousness equal status with my own; and I use this second-hand part of my consciousness to "put myself in your place." Accordingly my subject of study becomes differentiated into the contents of many consciousnesses, each content constituting a view point. Then there arises the problem of combining the viewpoints. . .

A. S. Eddington

TRANSCRIPTION (abridged)

The sentences are clear and straightforward enough. And the vocabulary isn't too bad. I guess I just have to stop after each one, let it sink in, and build to understanding that way.

I know right away what the main idea is. It's in the first sentence, but I don't yet understand it. Let's see. In my own words it's saying, "Things have to be in my head before I can think about them." Okay so far.

Next sentence translates: "Somehow part of what is in your head gets into mine, and I can think about that, too." Oh, I see. What I'm doing is rephrasing as I go along, sort of writing my own understandable version.

Third sentence: "I have to act as though what is in your head is just as good as what is in mine. I'm willing to accept that, but I'd hate to try to prove it. Anyway, once I accept it, I can think as you would in your place." (Walk a mile in your moccasins?) Gee, only two sentences to go.

Next to last: "All right. So I take in what I get from you and also from all sorts of people. I have lots of consciousnesses in my head, then, to think about. Each one is a particular slant on things.

Last: "How can I get them all fitted together?" In my own words:

The point is that I can only think about what is in my own head, but much of that comes from other people's legitimate views (somehow) and I have to fit them all together somehow.

The problem here, then, is to get the passage into the reader's own words. Once that is accomplished, it isn't hard to understand. The reader just thinks and rephrases as he goes along. As soon as he realizes what he needs to do, he goes about it purposefully.

Sample Four

How *do* you eat a giviak?

How to Eat a Giviak

Now it was winter, and Angutidluarssuk's giviak was frozen. He took his axe and started chopping up the icy stuff. Pink feathers and bird meat flew to all sides, while we watched in pious silence. At last the floor was completely covered with pieces of meat and blubber. Angutidluarssuk picked up a bite, tasted it, and threw it contemptuously away.

"Alas, as I told you: this is inedible. Possibly I have, through an oversight, filled the skin with dogs' dung. Possibly it is only my absolute ignorance about how to make a giviak that has caused this mistake! If you would show me a kindness, you would leave me now so that I could be alone with my shame!"

Upon this invitation, we started in. It tasted good the moment I got it in my mouth. But I had to be taught how to eat this remarkable dish. As long as it is frozen, you just chew away. You get feathers and bones in your mouth, of course, but you just spit them out. Frozen meat always has an enticing taste, and as it dissolves in the mouth, you get the full aroma of the raw fermented bird. It is incredible how much you can down, unbelievable how hard it is to stop. If you happen to come across a fully developed egg inside a bird it tastes like a dream. Or the liver, which is like green cheese. Breast and drumsticks are cooling and refreshing. It was late before we were full , and there was then about half of the giviak left. This was put up on one of the bunks to thaw for later use.

When we had had some sleep, we started the second part of the feast. The giviak was now so much thawed that the little auks tasted entirely different, and it was possible to eat them in a new way. Whole birds could now be pried loose from the compressed mass, and when that is the case, great elegance can be demonstrated while enjoying them. A man with *savoir-vivre* holds the bird by the legs with his teeth.

Then he strokes it with both hands, thus brushing off the feathers that have already been loosened by the fermentation. He brushes his hands together to remove all feathers, whereupon he turns the bird and bites the skin loose around the beak. This can then be turned inside out and pulled free of the bird without letting go of its legs. The eater then sucks the whole skin into his mouth and pulls it out again, pressing his teeth slightly together. In this manner, he gets all the delicious fat sitting inside the skin. Taste is, as we know, an individual matter, but this one—I dare guarantee—can become a passion.

When the skin is free of fat, you bite it free around the bird's legs and swallow it in one piece. The breast is eaten by biting down on each side of the bone, and the bone can then be thrown away. This bares the innards, and you can enjoy the various parts one by one. The blood clot around the heart has coagulated and glues the teeth together, the liver and gall bladder have a spicy taste, while the bitter aroma of the intestines reminds one of lager beer. When these parts are consumed, the rest—wings, backbone, and pelvis—is taken into the mouth and thoroughly chewed.

Such delicacies were always served in Angutidluarssuk's house.

From *Peter Freuchen's Book of the Eskimos*

SNAGS

Some readers get sidetracked on what *giviak* means. The "assignment" is to find out how to eat one, not to say what one is. Some readers immediately impose their own taste and decide the meal is gruesome. The author thinks it is delicious, but they totally ignore that and don't give him a chance. The task is to find out how to eat it, not to pass judgment. To read accurately, first you have to see it as the author sees it. Then you can go ahead and vomit if you want to.

The real reading problem in "How to Eat a Giviak" is in visualizing the process. It is the same one you have in reading how to bake a cake or how to install a washer. The thing to do is to zip through once to get the general idea. Here, you see there are two major parts: when it is frozen and when it is thawed. Imagine yourself going through each step. Try to "see" yourself doing it. You have understood the process when you can describe the steps in your own words. Of course, the best way to check your understanding is to install the washer, bake the cake, or eat the giviak.

This writer has never been able to visualize what exactly is done in the following two sentences. Thus, though he may know a great deal about how to eat a giviak, he cannot say he knows how completely.

. . . *whereupon he turns the bird and bites the skin loose around the beak. This can be turned inside out and pulled free of the bird without letting go of its legs.*

We have tried to visualize this step but without complete success.

By the way, even though you don't have to know, you can get a pretty good idea of what a giviak is from the context (surrounding words). From paragraph two you see it is some kind of skin filled, not with dogs' dung, but with birds (paragraph one), feathers and all. The birds are small, are called auks, and are fermented. The kind of skin is not mentioned; it is a seal skin left full of auks to ferment in the shade during the summer. The auks are caught in nets and killed by pressing the thumb against the rib cage, stopping the heart.

"I see what browsing through a reading right at the beginning does for you: It lets the mind open itself to the information without overwhelming it. Then, a bit later when the mind has got itself used to the way the information is coming across, you can read through smoothly. "

A student

BFAR: A STUDY-READING METHOD

The BFAR method puts the preceding ideas into an orderly pattern useful for any reading assignment, even for novels. Don't do more than is needed for your purpose (you might even skip some steps). But, if you bother at all, never skip step four.

BFAR Study-Reading Method

Browse.   Find out what has to be done to accomplish your purpose.

Focus.   Get the picture. Zip through for main ideas (or whatever else your purpose requires)**without stopping or taking notes.**

Absorb.   Go back and mark key ideas. Clear up any confusion, but only if you need that idea. You don't have to master every single thing you run across.

Reinforce.   Put what you just read in your own words, either by writing it or by explaining it to someone else.

THUS:

Browse.

Browse through the chapter, getting the feel of it, noting the main headings, looking at pictures. Skim summaries and questions provided. Decide how much time is needed and how hard it is. Break the chapter (or book) into manageable lumps. Set time limits for each lump including time for browsing, absorbing, and reinforcing. **Always allow a little less time than you think you need.** It will keep you alert and gradually speed up your work. This part is like planning for a backpacking trip. Decide now what you will look for in your first read-through. The surer you are of your goal the easier it will be to look for it. **Always have a purpose.**

Focus.

Read through once quickly without stopping or taking notes. Be alert and responsive to the writer's ideas, as though you were having a conversation. Question whenever it feels right, but act as though someone wants you to understand something. Be open to it.

Get a general idea of the main points—in a chapter, usually three to five—and the reasoning. Skip or skim anything you know you don't need. Don't worry about complete mastery yet.

Absorb.

This is where you work the material into your memory banks. Go back and find the main idea. Highlight or underline it, the **key words only.** Put some sort of outline notation in the margin (I, II, III, etc.) Underline supporting ideas if they seem important or might help you brush up for quizzes (A, B, C, etc.) Mark just enough to trigger your memory when you review for tests later. Too many or too few notes will just waste your time.

Reinforce.

Before you take a break, be sure to test your understanding by telling someone or writing **from memory** what you have just read and absorbed. Is it clear? Skim back over any fuzzy material. Some students write the gist in the bottom margin. Marking and writing in the text gets rid of the need for a separate notebook. An outline in the margin is right there for easy review.

Give yourself a **reward** before going on to the next lump (take a little break; have some coffee; play with the dog; have a snack).

But, if you skip the reinforce **step, you will forget most of what you have read by the next day and will have to do it all over again.** If you do reinforce now, brief brush-ups are all that will be needed.

MARKING AND MAKING NOTES IN BOOKS

Get all your notes for a subject in one place, if possible. Make the fewest you can get by with. "Simplify, simplify!" Compress and combine wherever you can. The less junk, the clearer and freer your mind will be. You have probably seen texts with every line highlighted in yellow or neatly underlined—with a ruler! Whoever did that has probably long since had a breakdown. It is the sort of behavior that gives college a bad name.

Too many notes are confusing. You end up having to re-do the studying you should have finished in the first sitting. There are two purposes for marking a text. First, it helps you see how a chapter is put together, the organization, the main and supporting points, and what is just repetition or padding. (Mark key ideas in the **Absorb** step of BFAR.) Second, once marked, your key ideas are in the right place for review and brush-ups. You don't want to have to search for them. Make them stand out. Mark just enough to trigger your memory of the pattern and situation. Two words where one will do is fifty per cent inefficient.

For example, assume you will be tested a week from now on the paragraph above. What is the least you could mark so that next Thursday night you could glance swiftly at the paragraph and trigger all you need for the quiz? How you do this is up to you. It is for your own use. Don't try to make it just like someone else's.

Here is one possibility. The bold print is the part that would be underlined or highlighted.

marking purposes

Too many notes are confusing. You end up having to re-do the studying you should have finished in the first sitting. There are **two purposes for marking** *a text. First, it helps you see how a chapter is* I *put together, the* **organization,** *the* **main and supporting points,** *and what is just repetition or padding. (Mark key ideas in the Absorb* II *step of BFAR.) Second, once marked, your key ideas are in the* **right place for review** *and brush-ups. You don't want to have to search for them. Make them stand out. Mark just enough to trigger your memory of the pattern and situation. Two words where one will do is fifty per cent inefficient.*

The marked phrases stand out and the rest fades back. For this reader just that much would be plenty. He reviews with the chapter open. First he sees "Marking purposes" and sees the I and II. He tries to remember. If he can't, he glances to the left. Oh, yes. **Organization** and **review.** If he still feels shaky, the information is right there where he needs it. He can browse or study anything that has faded.

The same procedure can be used for a whole chapter. First, see just how much has to be remembered or mastered to satisfy the teacher's requirements. Then, in the **Absorb** step, try to remember without help, "What's the writer getting at? How many subpoints? What are they?" Underline or highlight phrases you need and key them to indicators you put in the margin (I II, III, A, B, C). Browse or study any point still unclear and then mark its key phrase. This procedure highlights key points and shows the relation. Also, as you know, this same system is used for committing information to your memory storage system.

Refinements

The following extra touches are not essential, but they are good for helping you spot your notes.

To make your marginal cues more useful, write key words or phrases in the margin (as we did in the example above). There are usually three to five in a chapter, and usually they are in bold print. Be stingy, though. You want the skeleton to stand out plainly.

Or think of a figure of speech, something you can "see" that grabs the mind and sticks. *What is it like? Marking* is like *mapping* a route on a road atlas. So, if you want to think of the right way to mark a chapter, just think of it as *mapping* your way through the "territory." Use what works, any good memory cue from Chapter One.

For your own use, anything else you feel like jotting down is up to you. As you no doubt know, many thinkers "talk back" to an author in the margin or extend the idea there. But that is education, something you do for the joy of using your mind. You can do that once you knock off the assignment— which in most cases only wants the facts.

You can put class notes in the margin, too, alongside the appropriate passage. More on that in Chapter Four.

Rewrite

Once you are sure you know the gist and have marked what is important, put it in your own words in the bottom margin. Work toward getting all the essentials in the fewest words. When this crucial step is neglected, memory fades rapidly. Active restructuring of new material in your own words, however, dramatically improves retention. Only brief touch-ups are needed thereafter. So make it a fixed practice to go back and map or mark your assignment and never take a break until you sum up the material in your own words. Try it a few times and you will experience a remarkable improvement in understanding and retention.

MAPPING

If you have trouble visualizing the pattern of a reading assignment, you might try sketching a **map** on scratch paper during the **absorb** step. Any kind of picture is okay. This chapter
might look something like this:

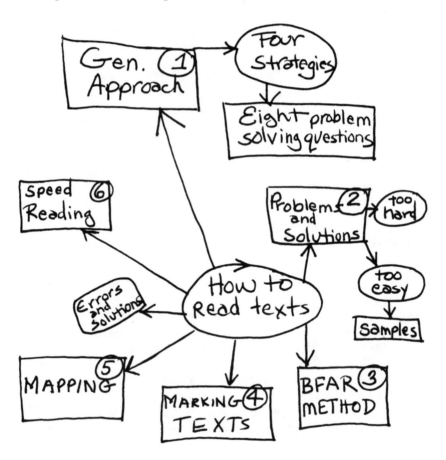

When you are working on any section of a chapter, such as the BFAR method in this one, you can make a map of it in the same way. And if you prefer you can put in a map instead of a summary at the end.

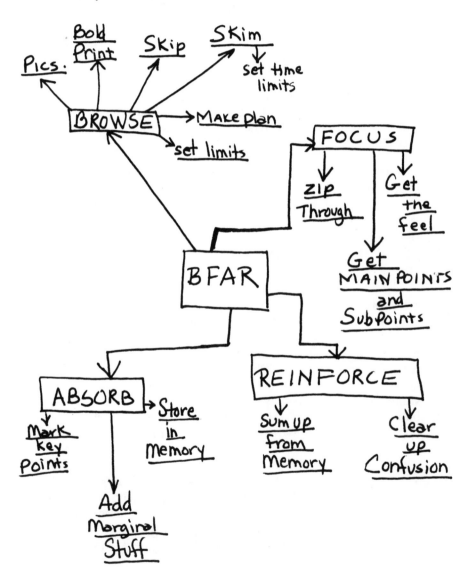

TEN ERRORS IN READING AND SOLUTIONS

Some problems are not in the print but in our approach. Here are some common mistakes people make and some countermeasures. In general, always read for meaning and always fit new material into your existing structure.

● **Incomplete or weak understanding.** We quickly read through how to do something or how something works and it seems clear enough. But when it comes time for us to demonstrate our grasp, we can't—how to eat a giviak, for example.

Solution. Explain it in your own words to someone else, preferably someone who doesn't already know it. Let him ask questions. Teachers are well aware that **teaching someone else is one of the best ways to learn.**Many have said they did not really grasp their subject until they started teaching it. To teach well, you have to understand both the pattern and the details. If you can't find someone to tell it to, write it out or draw a sketch or both.

● **Going too far.** For example, in the first paragraph of this chapter is the sentence, "Wasting time on school books numbs the mind and senses and thus retards education." Some readers are bound to broad jump to the conclusion that the writer doesn't think you should read textbooks at all. That is going too far and misses his point. He means that any book should be read efficiently. He doesn't like the self-defeating habits that go with wasting time. He admires well-written textbooks and wishes there were more of them.

Solution. Don't draw conclusions from isolated sentences. Think of the whole context in the paragraph and in surrounding ones. Reviewing and rephrasing help eliminate this habit.

Another problem is the reader's mind set. Some will see something they don't like (or do like) and let their initial guess dominate the entire reading. Suspend judgment and let the passage speak its mind. Agree or not only when you are sure of what it says.

● **Including too much.**   You see children doing this. "Daddy's outside shaving the windows." The child includes too much in the meaning of the word *shave*. Or he calls any male *daddy*.

Solution.   In reading try to take only as broad a meaning from a word as the writer intends. Draw his meaning from the whole paragraph or chapter. (He may *want* to expand the meaning of the word *shave*.)

● **Including too little.**   We all acquire meaning from our experience. Commonly, college students have a narrower meaning for many words than is intended in their books and classes. The meaning worked well enough in their former environment but not now. For example, many people think *to criticize* means to find fault with, but in the college community and in texts it usually includes examining both good and bad aspects.

Solution.   Again, the full context will probably show that a broader meaning is intended. And keep in mind **a major job of getting educated is to realize that additional possibilities still exist for all concepts.** Stay open to them.

● **Too rigid.**   When our minds are made up, it is impossible to read clearly. We don't let the writer get a word in. We just *know* we are right about Nixon or open marriage.

Solution.   Get used to alternatives. Be willing to change your mind when new evidence appears. Practice trying to see other views (even if it is only a game at first). **Ability to tolerate and appreciate more views is a second major task of getting educated.**

● **Wrong scheme.**   Picking up the wrong cues can lead a reader to misread an entire passage. For example, students in an English class were missing the point of a passage about how human views of right and wrong would stand up if viewed from a distant star. Then the teacher noticed the first sentence mentioned Zen and Christianity. Readers were discounting the main point and were sidetracked on Zen instead.

Solution.   Browsing and focusing help, and checking your conclusions by a quick rereading should reveal the error. Discussions with others is good, too. Being alert to this natural tendency is the best defense, though. (The teacher cut out the sentence on Zen and Christianity and students had no further trouble with the passage.)

● **Missing the pattern.**   This comes from not setting one's purpose in advance. When we read passively, just what is assigned, the tendency is to read masses of seemingly isolated details. We end up not knowing what it is all about. Since learning is actually restructuring one's inner picture of the world, such an approach is senseless. The material will not stick.

Solution.   Get an overview before you read, and mark the structure after you do.

● **Rules and directions too hard.** If you can't make head or tail of explanations, it may be the wording is too general or too abstract. There may be no recognizable images for you to see. In ordinary life, rules usually come *after* experiences. We plunge in, and afterward the description is perfectly clear and easy to remember.

Solution.   When you realize the explanation is not clear, go immediately to an example, anecdote, or problem. Even if you don't quite understand, the explanation will make much more sense because you will have something concrete in mind as you work through the rule or instruction. For example, when you get a bicycle to assemble, play with the parts, roughly figure out where they are likely to go and when. *Then* read the instructions.

● **Passage not clear.**   A passage may become so involved and complicated a reader gets lost.

Solution.   Work through it **out loud**. Visualize the steps as you go. For example, while he worked on his back behind our new clothes dryer, the installer had my wife read the directions to him out loud. And he made her *go slow*.

● **Instructions not clear.**

Solution.   As above, if they are causing trouble, read instructions out loud. Try this with assignment instructions, too. And put them in your own words. **Slow down.**

SPEED READING

Indirectly, this chapter has been devoted to increasing your speed. Practice with the BFAR method will noticeably cut down the time you spend to get what you need. Your speed, of course, will vary with your purpose, but BFAR allows for that.

Most people read 250 to 300 words per minute on the average. And they read everything at the same rate and read every word. You can see that is not a bright thing to do. We talk at about 150 to 180 words per minute. So this average isn't much faster than talking. Your rate ought to vary from about 120 WPM, when you have to think as you go, to 800 or better, when you are skipping and skimming familiar stuff. Your average can be over 450 with practice. If you want, you can very likely learn to read comfortably every word of material that is just right for you at about 400 words per minute. You could easily reach that speed with a couple of weeks of short daily practice.

A Simple Technique

● **First, use BFAR.** Once it is a habit it will come easily.

● **Second, every day read for a while, fifteen or twenty minutes, a little faster than is comfortable.** Read something, a novel probably, that is just right for you. Figure out how long it takes you to read a page in that book at your present rate. Then keep an eye on your clock or use a timer to pace yourself—a little faster each day. (Words per minute is the number of words you read divided by the number of minutes it took you.)

You can pace yourself by moving your hand across the page just under the line you are on.

That is all there is to it. Your speed is a habit and, as with running, you can get faster by getting in shape. Slower speeds allow bad practices: Reading word by word and missing the main idea; passive fooling around; skittering back over material you could have gotten the first time (called *regressions*); dwelling on words you could grab at a glance. But just by speeding up, you can get rid of most of these or greatly reduce their effect.

BFAR shows you what to skip and skim, so you can actually get meaning from some material three or four times as fast. You won't be reading every word, but, anyway, you should do that only when every word is important.

VOCABULARY AND SPEED

Should you take a crash vocabulary course to speed up your reading? It is true that too small a vocabulary can slow you down. You could breeze right along otherwise.

Normally the problem takes care of itself. Most adults know about 50,000 words. But college sophomores are estimated to recognize three or four times that many. How do they learn so many words in two years? It is not from poring over dictionaries and underlining every new word in their texts. Their new environment is so full of experiences and ideas never before encountered that words to describe them naturally follow, thousands and thousands of them. Most students hardly notice it happening. Going to college is like going to a foreign country. If you allow yourself to go native, you will soon be speaking the language.

Don't be alarmed if college texts seem foreign at first. They *are*. Gradually they will start to make sense. Read for meaning and pattern; look for ideas. You can get what you need despite the word barrier, and, bit by bit, the vocabulary will clear up. (Tactics for plowing through dull material appear earlier in this chapter.)

Vocabulary Building.

If you have the spare time (who does?), working on a larger vocabulary can pay off. Norman Lewis' *Word Power Made Easy* is a good paperback. Mostly, though, a vigorous curiosity about words is effective enough. In your spare time, for the fun of it, notice the origins of words, their root meaning and their affixes. Browse your dictionary. Notice etymology (the origins and history of words). See how words are related to each other. Everyday words are likely to originate from Anglo Saxon or Middle English. *Daisy,* for example, is from Middle English *daies ie* (day's eye), the sun. Textbooks have a high concentration of words of Latin and Greek origin. When you break them down, they are not too formidable. Every time you do look up a word, put a check in the margin. Usually, you will not end up with more than three checks for each word.

So the natural way is best: Be open to new ideas and the words will follow. Develop a curiosity about words and have fun with them in your spare time. Finally, a well-written vocabulary book can help. The more words you recognize, the easier and quicker you can get through the print and the easier it will be to understand the ideas.

DEMYSTIFYING COLLEGE READING

Anyone of ordinary intelligence who can read at sixth- or even fifth-grade level can get necessary meaning from a college text. Once one knows how to decode print, success owes more to problem-solving experience than to reading skill. Reading *is* problem solving. Consciously noticing one's own processes gradually builds a background of alternatives. Knowing we have these alternatives gives us the confidence to persist. Confidence, persistence, and knowledge of alternatives are basic to success. They reinforce each other. Since most people have succeeded in some area of their lives—music, carpentry, tennis, mechanics, the Peace Corps—they already know how to solve problems. **The game is one of focusing, gathering more information, reconsidering, setting and changing goals. It includes possibilities, probabilities, pay-offs, and penalties.** Getting meaning from print depends on realizing how similar the two processes are and on applying the same techniques

BFAR (**Browse, Focus, Absorb, Reinforce**), each with its obvious substeps, reminds a reader to use his prior problem-solving knowledge. Since life itself is nothing else but problem solving, it makes sense to welcome and enjoy the challenge.

4

Taking Classes
and
Doing Assignments

IN THIS CHAPTER

SYNOPSIS

One of the most difficult learning environments is the conventional classroom. Counter-productive methods promote grade-lowering habits and absenteeism. Students who are alert and imaginative in other settings are listless during lectures, their minds wander, and they retain little of what is presented. This chapter suggests methods for succeeding in a failure-oriented atmosphere and for completing assignments efficiently.

The first section shows how to build productive habits in the classroom. A slightly modified BFAR problem-solving method tells how to handle lecture classes. It includes how to warm up, where to sit, how to talk without fear, the kind of notes to take, and how to stay awake.

A trouble-shooting section provides alternatives for overcoming the most common classroom difficulties, including personality conflicts, difficult subject matter, too much homework, boredom, class-hour conflicts, and prejudice.

The second half of the chapter concerns assignments and how to do them in the least time and with the least anxiety. A method is given for analyzing your use of time and for developing a practical schedule. First you analyze your present habits and then deliberately schedule productive ones. Then follow refinements for BFAR. Included are six concentration tips and five ideas for breaking daydreaming habits.

The summary reminds the reader of his natural learning ability and emphasizes the value of deliberately applying it in artificial surroundings such as the classroom. As has been stressed throughout this book, conscious awareness of one's power to cope with adverse conditions and the building of those strengths into reliable habits is the key to success with assignments and classes. But, even more important, these very strengths are needed for one's own self-education.

THE PASSIVE CLASSROOM

Even though research shows lecturing to be one of the least effective teaching methods, most classes are still conducted with students seated passively in rows and the teacher in front doing all the talking. Lecturing is so ingrained we have actually seen a teacher droning on at four silent and polite students seated in front of him. Another arranged the seats in a circle but lectured all the same.

Most college teachers know little about the findings of educational research. Most institutions accept knowledge of subject as sufficient qualification for teaching. The old, counter-productive methods persist. Fear—"You'll be tested on this"—is still used to motivate students, even though positive reinforcement is known to result in better learning with fewer neuroses. Classrooms still try to transmit information even though it could be acquired better elsewhere. The structure encourages passivity and absenteeism. In general, antiquated, ignorant practices actually promote dullness. Passive mental habits lead to C's or worse for the majority of students. (We know from Bloom and others that 95 per cent of these same students can succeed in other settings.)

But five per cent do succeed. They are not necessarily smarter. And they often work and worry far less than C students. Any normal person, recognizing the structure and using it to advantage, can get top grades in less time and with less work than he probably takes now. All it requires are some new habits, some easy to acquire, some taking practice and planning. In fact, **the key to success in class and in doing assignments is habit.**

HOW TO TAKE CLASSES

If you pay attention, attend every class, and be sure to take every quiz and test, you can almost guarantee yourself a C or better—even if you do nothing else outside of class.

The reason is that most teachers still see themselves as transmitters of information and feel guilty if they don't "cover" in class everything they think is important. For them, the text is back-up material. And you can be pretty sure their tests will focus on what they talk about. If you don't intend to study at all, make sure you select teachers like this and apply good techniques in class. On the other hand, if you love the subject and want to master it, these same techniques will get you all the important information, and you will waste the least amount of time. And that will free you to go after your education.

Don't try to change twelve years of habits overnight, though. Build new habits one step at a time. Enjoy the challenge, and don't take it too seriously. It is pitiful to watch the inevitable collapse of a massive self-improvement program, usually about one week later. Suggested tactics are intended to be absorbed gradually at your own pace. Use what you can now and add on as you go. Your own temperament is your best guide; build on that.

Teach yourself to pay attention while you are there and you will be able to complete most of your work right in class. Occasional review could be enough to get by.

How to Pay Attention: The BFAR Method

With minor adjustments BFAR (Chapter Three, page 103) works for a lecture as well as for a text. You don't have to master a new system. But you do have to have *some* system. Most students just let the fifty minutes happen to them. Let the **B** stand for **Before. Focus, Absorb,** and **Reinforce** are fine just the way they are. Make necessary allowances for the message being spoken instead of printed.

Try to anticipate the lecture pattern, find the teacher's point, listen for subpoints and supporting details as you go. Then write in your own words a nutshell gist before you leave the room.

THUS:

BEFORE.

Get ready mentally. Speakers usually say right away what the point and approach for that session will be. If not, you can usually figure it out. Often they announce tests and assignments, too. But most students take a while to get settled (if ever), and by then the teacher is already into the first point and the game is almost lost. The lag is natural but costly. The solution is to develop a new habit: **Get ready** *before* **the teacher starts in.**

● **Avoid taking classes with old friends.** Be cold blooded. These pals will expect you to keep your old behavior. They will distract you, and you will perform for them. Your boy friend or girl friend will be an even worse nuisance: Whispering, note passing, casting eyes back and forth, erotic day dreams, showing off. Right? Five years from now they will have disappeared and you will be left holding your lousy grade card. If you want a study partner, find someone new in the class.

● **Sit in a conspicuous place as close as you can to the teacher.** This *forces* you to stay awake during monotonous sessions and requires less self-nagging. Avoid sitting near windows or attractive people. Other things being equal, students who sit closer to the teacher get better grades. You can hear better and there are few distractions— around you and inside you.

● **Take care of preliminaries.** Go to the toilet ahead of time. Don't overeat so you fall asleep or starve so your stomach growls the whole time. Get there a little early so you will have time to get a bead on things. Lay out your stuff. Each time bring what you do need or are likely to need. Put everything else off your desk where it won't distract you.

● **Settle nagging concerns.** Realize you can't do anything about your personal problems during the next fifty minutes anyway, so make a note to yourself or keep a reminder list.

Avoid encounters right before class. Break off with your sweetheart when you have plenty of time to be upset, certainly not between classes.

● **Work on these habits until they are automatic.**

FOCUS.

● **Find the structure early.** Get your mind in gear by reviewing notes from last time. Anticipate the likely topic for this session. If there is a chapter in your text on this topic, browse the bold print and pictures. Picture the speaker's structure, the sooner the better. Visualize: Diagram or map the lecture. Keep it loose, though, in case you guess wrong. You need some sort of skeleton to flesh out. The lecture will seem a hodgepodge otherwise. Even a miserable lecturer hopes to make some point, though you may have to be very alert to find it.

Since you can't reread a lecture, you will have to adjust your guesses about the meaning as you go along. What is the teacher's point? Later, reconsider. Does your guess still seem right? Should you adjust it? Only by watching the plan can you distinguish what a speaker thinks is important. Otherwise it all sounds equally unimportant, just a long list of facts.

● **Judge only when you must.** Listen sympathetically, not because you like the speaker but because you can't get the real message any other way. Pretend it is a conversation with a friend and you want to see it as he does. If you take a position before you hear a lecturer out, you could easily filter an entire talk through your bias screen. If you still want to, do the hatchet job afterward. In most classes you will lose. Most lectures are intended to be remembered, not evaluated or thought about. Grade getters keep the teacher's goals clear and avoid emotional involvement. If you can make your argument stick, most teachers will resent you, especially if you challenge their ideas in class. Unless you are sure that reflective thought is also the teacher's goal, mull over, restructure, and sort out ideas on your own time. It is what education is all about, but schools rarely give grades for it. If you happen to have the good luck to find such a school, you and everyone else will know it.

ABSORB.

Just as a text does, a speaker usually has one topic to present and three to five or so subdivisions. At first, watching for these will be difficult but with practice you will learn to recognize cues and will even learn tricks for staying awake, not because it is virtuous but because you don't want to slog through the whole thing again and because you won't even get the chance. Most courses center on the class lectures, so it is self-defeating to be passive in class. And passivity is addictive. As a countermeasure make a game of finding structure anywhere: in sermons, in TV documentaries, and so on. After five or six tries you will begin to see it is more fun than dozing.

Usually, a lecture will have enough relationship to your own experience that you can find connections. Mentally translating the material into your own language will help you remember it, and it will make more sense.

● **To stay awake, say something.** If you have ever offered a comment, asked or answered a question, you know that for a while your attention is sharply heightened, even after the laser moves on to someone else. So, to keep alert, deliberately get your voice into the arena. Every time your mind begins to wander, ask something or offer a comment. Use this tactic sparingly, however. Don't make a pest of yourself. There is usually plenty of room for legitimate questioning and commentary. Often the question you ask is the one someone else was thinking but was afraid to ask. Use the technique just enough to make yourself feel a part of the dialog and not a bystander.

● **Reduce fear in steps.** Gradually overcome fear of talking by starting with nonthreatening opportunities. If the teacher asks the date or where he left off, you can at least answer those questions safely. That way you get to hear your voice in the room. Do that every chance you get; speaking up will begin to feel okay. Do whatever you can to get comfortable. Get used to the teacher. Visit his office so that he won't seem so inhuman. If you can get up the courage, tell him about your trouble talking in class. As we have said several times in this book, there are lots of solutions. Counselors can suggest some, but mainly just think about ways to make yourself feel more at home.

● **Be noticed.** Take every advantage you can get. Students who hide, keep their heads down, and avoid the teacher are begging for a lower grade. The front office questions too many high grades and most teachers will try hard to make their grade sheets look good. Guess what happens to borderline students they don't know.

● **Show an interest.** Make eye contact, but don't stare. Just let the teacher see you are responsive. Use your body language just as you would in a conversation. Let your face be expressive. A room full of poker-faced students is pure hell for a teacher. You want the person who gives the grades to feel friendly and helpful. Like any other animal, teachers can be conditioned to behave well or poorly. Students have tremendous power to affect class atmoshpere. So lean forward, ask enough questions and make enough comments to keep your hand in. But don't hog the show.

● **Make sure the teacher knows you and knows your name.** When you meet out of class, remind him, "I'm Steve Swenson in your 10:00 class." Be sure to visit his office within a few days after classes start—for any reason. Your real purpose is to make sure he knows who you are ("I'm Kathy Luttner in your 2:00 class") and to find out more about him. Anonymity and low grades go together. So make sure you are not forgotten. You can just go through the motions of showing interest, but you will feel much more alive if you really do get curious. If you simply can't, at least don't be obvious about it.

● **Take notes.** Taking notes won't make you remember better, research shows, but it can help you pay attention while you absorb the pattern and key ideas. You stay on track easier. Notes can also provide safe storage for later memorization. **The fewer notes the better.** Since you can't listen and write, too, just get down a word or phrase for key ideas to trigger the context later. Figures of speech aid recall better than technical jargon. Identify relationships by your own marking system, indentations, spacing, or a map. **Abbreviate.**

If you try to copy everything word for word—and many stenographers do—you might as well stay home and send a tape recorder instead. You won't get much meaning from the lecture and you will have to go over the whole thing again at home. Get key ideas, details the teacher emphasizes, and anything that will help you remember. Leave space so you can fill in later as needed.

REINFORCE.

You know how memory fades, so take one or two minutes to reinforce your understanding before you leave the classroom. Otherwise stimuli outside the door will wash out most of your work and you will have forgotten even an interesting lecture by bedtime. Most people ignore this step, but it is a bad investment to waste fifty minutes just to gain two.

While still in your seat write from memory in your own words the gist of what you just learned. Check over your notes to resolve any confusion or grab the teacher before he gets away.

Within twenty-four hours review again by rewriting your notes in a briefer form. Use memory devices. Convert material into "test" questions. If the lecture parallels a text chapter, transfer new material to the appropriate margins. Your book will then contain in one place everything you will need for review.

Trouble Shooting: Twelve Common Problems

1. WRONG TEACHER

First isolate the exact difficulty.

Vocabulary Barrier

● **If the lecture sounds like Greek, it could be either the teacher's personal vocabulary or the subject's terminology.** You have to figure that out first. If the teacher is showing off and class conditions are okay otherwise, BFAR should show whether you can get the main ideas despite the fog factor. If class is otherwise tolerable, you might as well pick up some new words.

● **Technical jargon is not usually a barrier.** Most school subjects involve a few new words undergraduates will need to know, but only majors in the field need to learn, gradually, the hundreds or thousands of special terms. A down-to-earth teacher using ordinary English can talk sensibly about highly complicated things—without watering down the concept. The best thing is to shop in advance for a serious teacher in the department who uses ordinary English and loves the subject. A pretentious teacher is more interested in how he sounds than in you or his subject. The previous semester sit in on classes, if allowed, and pick out the most reasonable teacher you can find. If you can't escape, you may have to get some other student to translate the lectures into your own language. Occasional questions about a term or concept may help, too.

● **Postponing a course a few semesters often works wonders.** A year from now your course-taking skills will be much improved. You will know the ropes and will be more familiar with the college vocabulary. You won't be the new kid on the block anymore.

- **If it is really necessary, drop or transfer.** Analyze what is happening cooly. If it is clear that things are not going to work out with this teacher, decide whether it would make sense to drop or try for a transfer to some other teacher. Give it a chance—lots of students chicken out too soon—but drop before penalty deadline (stated in your college catalog). If you try for a transfer, use tact. Thus, it is considered all right to want to change sections because of job hours but not because you think the teacher is a jerk.

- **Sometimes the teacher's meaning for certain words is different from yours.** Don't be surprised if he doesn't use some words the way you do. That should be expected. As you expand your experience of the world, just about every word in your vocabulary will expand its possible meanings. Additional possibilities exist for all concepts, all words. So let the context (the conversation in which it comes up) show you how the word is being defined. You may find words like *disinterested, catholic, ignorant,* and so forth being used in unfamiliar ways.

Boring Teacher

BFAR should help you keep awake. You can use the space between ideas to polish your map. Comments and questions can help keep you mentally active.

Offensive Teacher

Don't be too hasty. You will want to have someone who is challenging—just so he is not impossible. If you are too comfortable your mind will stagnate. So see if the personality conflict is within reason. So what if the teacher wears the same outfit all semester, has sex habits different from yours, twitches, lisps, or in some other way is human? See how many different types you can get along with. You learn more from people who are not like you. Thousands of students have started out hating a teacher and ended up with great respect—and even affection. And *vice versa*, of course. Stay open. Don't bulk too soon. Sometimes a few office visits help. Teachers are just like you and your friends, only older. But if it does turn out to be an impossible situation, drop or transfer.

2. SUBJECT TOO BORING

Use BFAR and get it all done in class so at least you can have some fun on your own time. The danger is in daydreaming and missing the one point made all hour. Watch for language and body cues. If it is a required subject, coolly aim for the grade. If it is not required, consider dropping. Boredom can ruin good study habits.

3. WRONG COUNTRY: APTITUDE

Does the course make you feel as though you are in a foreign country? There can be "personality conflicts" between students and subjects, too. Research suggests people can learn things whether they have an aptitude or not. They don't even have to have an interest. They just have to figure alternative routes to success. But if it is not required, don't take it. You will not go to hell just because you never made sense of chemistry or because the metaphoric language of poetry drives you crazy. No one knows very much at all when you think of all it is possible to know. Human knowledge is a thin layer of dust on the vast universe. So enjoy what your nature does guide you toward.

● **If the course is required, consider alternative texts, children's books, tutors, conferences with the teacher, plea bargaining, a different teacher, test analysis, chicken soup, some of the above, all of the above.** Foreign countries just take better travel agents.

● **If permitted, consider auditing the course before you enroll.** Twice through works wonders.

● **Or take it over.** Some schools allow you to try for a higher grade. Check your catalog or ask your registrar.

4. COURSE REQUIREMENTS TOO HEAVY

Analysis will show short cuts. BFAR can eliminate wasted motion—sometimes as much as two-thirds of the time usually spent. Course descriptions may list more than is really required or much of the busywork can be sidestepped. Rarely do you really have to read more than one extra book besides your text. Skimming and browsing are often enough to fill you in on other "required" books. Meet the requirements, but don't be the only one in class to do all the work and end up with only a C. **Find out what the teacher really wants and give that.**

A course should require about two hours of work for each session. Five three-unit courses would represent a forty-five-hour week. But BFAR skill can cut that down considerably. As you know, work load per course varies widely. Pre-plan. **If you can possibly arrange it, don't take more than one time-consuming course per semester.** Distribute no-work courses, too, so that your load is reasonable each semester.

5. JOB INTERFERENCE

A full-time student can handle a part-time job up to twenty hours a week. Research shows GPA drops beyond that. If you need the money, **consider fewer courses per semester.** Or try for a grant or scholarship at your financial aids office. Thousands and thousands of dollars go unclaimed every year. But if it gets too rough, why torture yourself? Twenty years from now an extra semester or so will make no difference. Figure out your priorities. Consider time and place as variables, not restrictions.

6. GENERAL BOREDOM

Take only interesting courses for a semester or so until your interest perks up. Or take a year or two off until you really want to be in college. Your parents no doubt will be disappointed,but almost all parents survive the trauma. Some even remember drop-out children in their wills.

7. ABSENTEEISM

After they flunk a few courses, most students who stick around develop regular attendance as insurance. You will be able to keep track of the general structure and will know teacher emphasis, tests, and dates. Regular attendance provides a stabilizing center around which to structure your other activities. The reduced anxiety is well worth fifteen hours or so in classes each week. Get so you don't even have to think about it.

8. INFLEXIBLE APPROACH

Subjects vary and call for different performance. So do teachers. A single, unbending approach to all classes is disastrous. Figure out what behavior changes you need to make for each course. Make a plan of attack and change it if necessary.

9. BAD CLASS HOUR

A veteran of the college battlefield once told us he deliberately took classes at inconvenient hours just to make the game interesting. However, if you really can't hack it, see if the teacher has another section you can attend. Swing-shift students have even been able to split their attendance among several sections, including evening classes.

10. THE FINE ART OF BUGGING THE TEACHER

Victimized teachers assign grades. So it is not exactly the most brilliant idea in the world to fool around in class or try to get the teacher's goat. Since grade-getting is the name of *this* game, put your imagination into strategies that pay off.

11. SACRED COWS: YOUR VALUED BELIEFS

If you are lucky, sooner or later college will upset all your settled ideas. Freshmen who cling blindly to their old values are in for rough times. Most entering students feel their assumptions threatened to some degree. However, if they stick around, they can expect a satisfying restructuring of their world view toward the end of their junior year. By their senior year most do become committed again—not necessarily to their old ideas— but with more openness and responsiveness. If a course steps on your toes, relax. Things will sort themselves out in time. You don't have to believe in alien ideas—just understand them.[1]

12. ASSIGNMENTS: CARRY A POCKET-SIZED NOTE PAD.

Try to get assignments exact. Do write instructions word for word. A turn of phrase here and there can make all the difference. Carrying a pocket-sized note pad with dated entries works. Make it a habit. **Include due dates.** Casual students never get the word.

Get to assignments as soon after class as possible while directions are still fresh in your mind. For example, students have found it helps noticeably to do math problems during the following hour while they can still remember the examples. Clear up any confusion yourself or check right away with your teacher, someone in your math lab, or another student.

---

[1] Perry, *Forms of Intellectual and Ethical Development.*

HOW TO DO ASSIGNMENTS

Many people spend all their time out of class doing school work or worrying about it. The work always expands to fill whatever time they set aside for it and slops over into everything else, too. They waste time on some subjects and have to skimp on others. Or they will sit staring at the books, doing anything they can to avoid getting started. Most students have no idea how long it takes them to master a history chapter or how fast they can read a page of *The Second Ring of Power*. They never made a schedule for themselves in their lives. Their feelings about studying vary from mild anxiety to hysteria. They also wonder why other people are getting the grades. Most students have never been taught or figured out for themselves how to handle assignments even though it is a fundamental school-game skill. Yet spending the least time and emotion on assignments is a rather simple skill to acquire.

To keep assignments in their place, you will need a plan and some new habits. The preceding chapters cover some aspects: memorization, mastering a textbook chapter, and getting ready for tests. This section shows some ways to square away your study time so you will have some left over for yourself. A full-time student ought to be able to spend a total of forty hours or less in school including class time. The more efficient one gets, the more that can be cut down. A vigorous young person ought to have better use for spare time than staring dolefully at a school book.

Make a Time-Place-Task Plan.

Sooner or later you will have to get your act together. Things that recur regularly, like assignments, must be done so automatically that no thought or effort is needed to get you going. Routines are lifesavers. They have a freeing effect on the spirit, and they can save you hours and hours. **To start, you will have to see how you are doing now. Then make a** schedule based on what you find out. Try it. And, finally, re-vise as needed until it fits. Then stick to it until one day you wake up and find it is a habit. From then on, school is a breeze.

FIRST WEEK: KEEP TRACK OF STUDY TIME.

Do things your usual way, but keep track on a chart of some sort, possibly like this one. (If this version suits you, there are three for your use in the back of this book.)

	TIME USE CHART		
	SUNDAY	MONDAY	TUESD
8			
9			
10			

> Keep this information on your chart:
>
> The exact amount of time for
>   each study session
> Where
> When
> Which book and how many pages
>   completed, or
> How many problems done
> Circle the times you could have
>   used but didn't.
> Abbreviate!

Analyze your chart.

At the end of the first week examine your chart and see what changes you want to make. Maybe you read history faster in your room than in the library or at night instead of in the morning. You must find out how long it now takes you to do a history assignment, how many pages you can do in a given time slot, when and where you do your best work for history. And you want the same information for each subject. If it is hard for you to concentrate on art history in the evening, maybe you could schedule your mechanical drawing for that time.

SECOND WEEK: FOLLOW A PRE-PLANNED TENTATIVE SCHEDULE.

Check over your first chart and plan your schedule for the second week. This time, decide in advance the amount you will try to do in a given time. Shoot for a little more each time. Build in just enough time pressure to keep you alert. Decide where the best place to do your physics is and when the best time is.

How soon does your attention drop off? Distribute the assignment over several sessions, if necessary. At least provide for short breaks between several manageable segments.

Lay out the whole plan on your chart. Then follow it. As the week progresses, you will need to revise for over-enthusiasm and to handle unforeseen snags. By the weekend you should have a pretty good grasp of what, when, where, to study and how much you can accomplish in one session. Your third week should be just about right.

Be sure to leave some free time for emergencies.

THIRD WEEK: MAKE A REVISED SCHEDULE.

Follow your revised schedule. You will need only slight adjustments.

FOURTH WEEK AND THEREAFTER.

Use your chart as needed. Keep one as many weeks as necessary to make the schedule a habit. Shortly, your routine will be part of you, like brushing your teeth and driving a car, and you won't need a chart. Regular work habits are essential to productive, untroubled life. Consider, for example, the approach of Jefferson biographer Dumas Malone, who spent over thirty-five years on his project: "My policy has always been in accord with my temperament: I don't press, but I keep eternally at it." He was in his mid-eighties at the time and had completed five award-winning volumes.

The Assignment Itself: BFAR

Never, never just wade in. Use BFAR. Make a plan and stick to it. This is the real secret for saving hours. Read over the assignment until you are sure what is required. Save any personal goals until you have satisfied the teacher's. Examine the whole task first. Then break it into manageable segments.

Above all, be sure to reinforce after each segment and at the end of the whole assignment. You want the material integrated inside yourself as much as possible. If you don't want to have to relearn the whole thing later, this step is crucial. So be sure to write from memory the gist of each segment and use memorizing techniques to fix in mind the key ideas. Put the material in the form of a test— just like one your teacher would make. If you don't reinforce, you will lose nine-tenths of all you learn.

REVIEW PERIODICALLY.

A good time is at the beginning of the next assignment for the same subject. Before you start the new one, take a minute or two to refresh yourself on what you learned the last time. Go over anything important you have forgotten. Review is a

good way to get your mind warmed up for the new assignment. Then, every week or so, check yourself again. And,
finally, do a general review the night before the test.

When you run into snags, use problem-solving tactics such
as those suggested in Chapter One, page 33 . Be confident that
every problem has many solutions. You have many resources
and many alternatives.

TEACH IT TO SOMEONE ELSE.

Teaching something is one of the best ways to learn it. It
forces you to be clear. See if you can make your spouse or a
friend grasp what you have learned. Make yourself available to
someone in class who needs help, or take turns with a study
partner explaining the concepts. (But work with someone else
only after you have worked through the assignment on your
own first. You are likely to get sidetracked otherwise.)

How to Concentrate

On their own, people concentrate naturally. Everyone has
experienced total effortless absorption, if not as adults, certainly in childhood. But those who can concentrate on school
work seem the exception. One reason is that much of what
goes on in school is not something students choose for themselves. There isn't any natural motivation. The only defense is
to apply a method deliberately. As you know from Chapter
One, without concentration, there is no way to get concepts
processed into our mental structure systems. When we are
passive, we waste time. We dawdle, appear stupid, and feel
that way. We have listed some preventive techniques for reading textbooks and for attending classes. In addition there are a
few more tactics you can use to help you concentrate out of
class.

HAVE A REGULAR PLACE TO STUDY.

Wherever you choose—you could have several spots—arrange it, if possible, so that you associate only efficient study habits with that spot. When you sit down, work begins.

● **Allow no distractions.** No picture of your favorite mountain lake or your sweetheart. Avoid picture windows.

● **Have nothing on your desk but materials you actually need for this time slot.** Put everything else off your desk and out of sight.

SET TIME AND QUANTITY LIMITS.

Before you start in, plan exactly how long you will take. Plan how much you will accomplish in that time. Your time-finder chart will give you guidelines. BFAR will show you where to break off for a breather. If the material will take an hour and you can only tolerate twenty minutes at a stretch, plan two short breaks. But, for reinforcement, complete BFAR on each part before each break.

STUDY SIMILAR SUBJECTS AT SEPARATE TIMES.

To avoid fatigue, try to distribute study over several sessions. If you must do more than one assignment in the same study session, make sure they are not similar. This practice will prevent your confusing the two in your mind, and the change will refresh you. Winston Churchill, for example, went from affairs of state to bricklaying or painting. Do literature and math together but not math and physics or literature and humanities. Your mind is capable of working all the time, provided it doesn't get bored.

● **Do difficult or boring subjects first.** Save the ones you enjoy for dessert.

REWARD YOUR SHORT-TERM GOALS.

Decide how many pages you should master or how many problems you should do in a time limit. Be firm. Set your clock. **If you achieve your goal, do something you like:** play your tapes, have some coffee, walk the dog. Otherwise, no reward. Some people keep charts of their progress day by day. They keep track of increases or decreases in number of pages completed, increases or decreases in how long they can stay with a subject without tiring. Keep your goals modest, and work one step at a time.

SETTLE DISTRACTIONS.

Don't get involved just before study time in fixing your car, arguing with your spouse, or doing your taxes. Settle their hash *after* you study. Instead, exercise a little or take a shower. You want your mind clear.

● **Train everyone to respect your study hour.** Either don't answer your door or let guests entertain themselves. There is no law that you must answer your phone. Pull the jack if you have to. **Hang a sign on your door or wear a garment that always means you are studying.** This is war. Your peace of mind and your grade are at stake. Once the assignment is finished, you will be a more agreeable companion.

ADJUST TO RANDOM NOISE.

When you are absorbed, most noise will notdistract you. Your study system should help keep you on track. With motivation, you could study in a boiler room. The real noise is usually inside us. Examine the distraction and choose one of the many alternatives for clearing it up.

For example, one student found she could study lying on the living room rug, her husband watching TV, the baby happily crawling around between them. (In the crib, he cried for attention.) When the student knew her family were contented, she could concentrate, even though there was a lot going on around her.

Conquer Mind-Wandering and Daydreaming

Don't let your mind associate study with daydreaming. It will do whatever you get it used to. Many minds automatically click off at the sight of a text. Try one or all of the following:

As soon as you realize you are daydreaming, put a ✔ in the margin. Keep a record of the number for each session. If there are more checks toward the end, study in shorter spans.

If preoccupied, stop, take a sheet of paper, and write out whatever is on your mind. Giving a problem full attention often frees the mind long enough to complete the assignment. Keep a reminder list. That helps, too.

Stand up and face the other way. Some psychologists recommend this tactic as a dramatic means of saying No to mind-wandering. It breaks the habit sharply. You won't have to get up very often.

To quiet your mind, meditate a minute or two. Just breathe at your normal rate and count each inhalation until you feel settled enough to continue.

If you get sleepy, work a while standing up. Prop your book on your dresser, or put your chair on the desk and prop the book on the seat.

SUMMARY: NATURAL AND ARTIFICIAL LEARNING ENVIRONMENTS

Without interference, most people learn easily and quickly. If they examined the accomplishments they take for granted, they would feel brilliant. They should. On this planet even the most ordinary human being is a phenomenal animal. School should reinforce our feeling of worth and ability, but it rarely does. Indeed, it seems almost designed to do the opposite. For most people it is at best a harmless bore and at worst a frightening, guilt-generating ordeal.

One reason is that teaching methods seldom make use of natural learning processes. They invite behavior which actually interferes with learning: passivity, daydreaming, timidity, lack of confidence, competitiveness, procrastination. College students have to realize this conflict and have the assurance to find on their own suitable approaches for taking classes and for studying.

Fortunately, their own learning success in other activities reveals excellent approaches which can be used with equal success in school. Using a problem-solving approach, they can handle lectures and assignments with relative ease. The BFAR method is a reliable way to include necessary steps: defining the problem, making and carrying out a plan, and checking over results.

The main barrier to success in class and at home is in not applying productive techniques often enough to establish habits. To reinforce habits is the first major task of college students. It is the only defense against four years of chaos. Once routines are established, students have plenty of time to pursue their own interests without anxiety.

5

Controlling School
Anxiety

ANXIETY

There are real fears and imagined ones. Most school dangers are imagined. There is little about the game that is worth the worry and fear most people experience. The few real threats are so slight or unlikely to happen that everyone in school ought to be perfectly comfortable and happy. But that is seldom the case. Real or not, anxiety functions just as if the threat really exists. As a result, people behave awkwardly in school and end up making their fears come true. To avoid stress, many skip classes, put off assignments, daydream, and sleep. And the more they do, the more threatening school seems. Anxiety affects grades as much as or even more than any other factor.

REAL DANGERS

This book shows how easy it is to control the few real dangers. It shows how to organize study time, how to read a text chapter, how to listen in class, how to remember, how to take tests. Once you know how the school game really works and learn some strategies, the real problems are trivial. For a person of normal intelligence there is nothing whatever to fear in school.

Whether they intend it or not, school institutions have made most people think otherwise. Rarely are students taught the skills for school success, those which really do affect their grades. In varying degrees, most have learned to fear teachers and classrooms, textbooks and tests. And even though they have learned coping tactics, many will continue their old emotional habits long after the danger is past. They need some methods for meeting these unreal anxieties head on.

ELIMINATING UNREAL FEARS

Fear of Tests

During a test, if you feel undue anxiety building up, there are several strategies—depending on how strong the feeling is. If you start to get too nervous over a difficult item or if it is taking too long, skip it and do some easy questions until your confidence is restored. You may gain some extra time to play with it. Review the tips suggested in Chapter Two: Get used to tests. Make up your own tests. Analyze earlier test items. Sit where you feel good. Jot down anything you fear you will forget. Schedule your time. Preview the test, read questions slowly, do easy ones first, review your work, use mnemonic devices. Persist, persist, persist.

Go with the Tension.

● **If you begin to tense up, consider going along with the tension.** That is, clench your fists tightly as you can, and tense up your whole torso, the shoulders, jaws, neck, stomach, your thighs and calves, too. (As much as you need.) Work on each part. Hold it a few seconds and let go. Try it again. The tension will drain out. You can usually do this, sitting at your desk without being noticed. Most people will be looking at their own test, not at you.

Quiet Your Mind.

● **If your mind is racing so that you can't concentrate, count your breaths for a minute or so.** Just sit at ease in your seat and breathe normally. But keep track of your inhalations, counting each one. Give your full attention to the counting. If you lose track, start over. Don't worry if thoughts intrude; just continue counting. This will quiet your mental chatterbox and allow you to focus on the test.

TECHNIQUES FOR OUTSIDE THE CLASSROOM

If you feel anxiety building up before a test, there are several things you can do. Get your body toned up. Some light exercise will help and possibly a shower, as we mentioned earlier. Don't get to class too early or too late. That can build up tension. Just give yourself enough time to get settled and get your materials laid out.

Give Yourself a Mental Massage.

● **Five to ten minutes just before a test, stretch out somewhere or sit where you won't be disturbed. Systematically "activate" your nerve endings.** Start with your big toes. Become conscious of them. As soon as you can really sense them, go on to your other toes, then to your feet and so on throughout your body, including your scalp. Not only does this exercise take your mind off your fears, but your body feels toned up. You feel good.

Mentally Rehearse the Fear Situation.

● **If your anxiety is more severe, try a step–by–step practice session before a test, going through your usual emotions.**

● **First get your body thoroughly relaxed by systematically tensing and relaxing your muscles as suggested above.**

● **Next imagine the steps leading up to the test.** Start far enough back to a point where you would be free of test anxiety. Then imagine yourself in each succeding situation and stay there until you feel comfortable. Since you are in a position of safety while you are imagining the process, you can control how you feel. You can gradually work through to the test itself, even individual parts of it, removing fear as you go. Take your time and come back for another rehearsal if necessary until you feel no discomfort or anxiety.

This approach is used with good results by psychologists to help people overcome all sorts of unreal panic: fear of snakes, height, elevators, sex, public speaking, and so forth. If test anxiety paralyzes you enough to spoil your performance, give it a try.

Meditate.

If you tend to be anxious about college—or life—in general, daily meditation of fifteen to twenty minutes will help calm you down. It should pay off in a clearer mind and a more comfortable feeling in school. Mainly, the exercise consists of sitting comfortably and paying attention to your breathing. It can be done anywhere, but a regular spot and time will help the process. Your goal is to become quiet in both body and mind.

● **Be comfortable but sit up straight, your back and head erect.** It is okay to cross your legs Amerindian fashion, if you wish, and lay one palm on the other in the Buddhist manner. Shift your weight around until the proper seating is found.

● **Keep your eyes open and focused.** A spot about two feet in front of you will do.

● **Let your breathing be natural and effortless.** Use the diaphragm.

● **Count each inhalation. When you reach ten, start over.**

As you count, your busy mind will wander to alien thoughts and it will be hard to concentrate. Don't try to force these thoughts out. Instead, when you realize they have crept in, just come back to the counting. Gradually, you will find it easier to focus and will be able to quiet yourself rapidly when the need arises.

SPECIFIC FEARS

Attack fears in a good problem-solving fashion. First determine what the fear is. Examine it carefully and redefine it, if necessary. Often something else is the real problem, not what you first identified. Decide if it is a real danger or only an imagined one. Then select a good tactic to get rid of it. Stay flexible. If one alternative doesn't work, try another.

Fear of Failure

If you finished high school with a C or better, this is an unreal danger. You have plenty of ability to meet college demands. Following just a few of the suggestions in this book will assure you a passing grade. Most undergraduate-level courses don't expect you to be an expert scholar. Teachers know it takes time for you to adjust. And most assignments will be within reason, more likely to be boring than difficult. Occasionally you may encounter an impossible course but not frequently enough to ruin you. Rarely is it lack of ability which makes people fail. Once you have had a few successes, you will begin to shed this fear.

Fear of Teachers

This is clearly an unreal fear. Look around at your fellow students. Some of them will be teachers. As you can see, there is nothing special about them. They have the full range of human strengths and weaknesses. They are not gods. Don't hand over power to them that they don't really have. One way to realize their humanness is to get to know a few out of class. Visit their offices. Don't refuse a cup of coffee in the cafeteria. Chat about other things than school occasionally. A good teacher will want you to feel at ease. Your ease makes teachers feel more comfortable, too, and the learning process flows better. Teachers are full of unreal fears, too. Many even fear students. One teacher listed in an article fifteen things he feared in the classroom. So try switching your perception around. See what you can do to make teachers feel safe. They will do a better job for you.

Fear of Talking in Class

This is an unreal fear, too. Several solutions are suggested in Chapter Four. Most people are afraid of looking foolish. But, if you examine it, either you are a fool or you aren't. More accurately, everyone is a fool some of the time. So what? Anyone who is afraid of making a fool of himself can never learn. Besides, it is vain to dwell on how one looks to others. As your own experience will show, people don't spend very much time thinking about the mistakes of others. They are much more concerned with themselves. An hour later they will not even remember a mistake was made or that you were the one who made it. How long do *you* remember when someone flubs it or who it was? Also keep in mind that your performance in class is almost never the main source of your grade. Any way you look at it, such fear is exaggerated.

● **If your fear is really powerful, try systematically desensitizing yourself in a step–by–step rehearsal process as de-**

scribed above. Before class, calm down your body and mind and then picture yourself closer and closer to the threatening situation until you imagine yourself actually asking a question or volunteering a comment. You will feel no anxiety. In class, having already talked successfully in your imagination, you will simply repeat what you have already done. Also, as mentioned earlier, get used to hearing your own voice in class when the pressure is off. Once you hear yourself speaking a few times, you will feel okay about it. Chatting before and after class with the teacher and students will help, too.

● **For severe stage fright, consult a counselor.** Many schools have programs expecially designed to help students overcome this fear. You are not alone.

Fear of the Unknown

There is a certain amount of sense in this fear—as long as it is used productively. It can keep you alert in new situations and help you watch for real danger. The future can be dangerous. One of these days it will kill you. But to let it keep you from trying new things would be to give up life. Your own experience shows that most of the time things work out all right. The more things you try out, the more you will feel at home.

Fear of Being Ignorant

If one were not ignorant, there would be no point in being in college. Only when we know we are ignorant and want to change can we begin to educate ourselves. Most people have been conditioned to be ashamed when they don't know something, but this shame keeps them ignorant. Complacency in one's ignorance or being too timid to inquire are the real dangers. Keep in mind that all knowledge is tentative. The most anyone knows is an infinitely small particle of what is possible. So we are all in the same boat.

Try a half-speed walk.

Do everything at half speed for ten minutes or so, walking, talking, even thinking. You will feel yourself quieting down. You will feel refreshed.

6

Taking Freshman English

WORDS ON PAPER

Conditions for freshman English vary tremendously from college to college, from teacher to teacher, and from student to student. So you will have to apply your best problem-solving techniques to meeting the requirement in your school. (And don't overlook the chance that you may be able to skip it altogether. Some schools do not require it or offer equivalency tests.) Traditionally, freshman English means composition—putting words on paper in some form agreeable to the teacher. Almost always your grade will depend on your writing, no matter what you are told. The problem narrows to one of producing words on paper to satisfy your particular teacher.

IF NECESSARY, DELAY TAKING THE COURSE

Despite a century of trying, schools know little about how to teach students to compose. One experiment revealed that high school students who did no writing at all for a year made just as much progress as those who had regular instruction. It is possible that a year of reading is as good training as any for learning to compose.

One purpose of freshman composition is to prepare students so that they can write better essays—short attempts at getting an idea onto paper—in their other courses. But there is some evidence that the reverse in more likely. **Taking other courses first could help you pass your English requirement.** So, if the idea of composition is too stressful your first semester, go ahead and postpone it. By the time you take the course you will know how to cope with most college problems, and your course work, reading, and conversation will familiarize you with the sort of discourse your college considers suitable. Just hanging around, you will become more skillful than you might expect.

Meanwhile, you will have a chance to decide what sort of assistance you might need, and you can use the time to identify a compatible teacher. **The right teacher can make all the difference.** Ask around and sit in, if possible. Find out how much work is required. In most schools there is a wide range. Also examine A and B essays of your acquaintances. Read the teacher's comments. See what various teachers consider good writing.

Once you are enrolled in class, if you have problems that have to do with class in general and are not specifically composition difficulties, check the trouble-shooting tips in Chapter Four, page 127. Minor tinkering may be all that is needed. Save drastic measures as a last resort.

HOW TO WRITE FOR FRESHMAN ENGLISH

Most English teachers were literature majors in school. Few have had much more than a course or two in composition beyond the freshman course. Even fewer have been instructed in how to teach writing. While they may indeed be able to describe what is attractive in a finished composition, many may not know exactly how to persuade students to compose such a paper. They are like native speakers of French who know when what they say sounds okay, but they may not be able to explain why. Once students understand this, they can use what English teachers do know to their advantage.

Most schools will expect you to write a two- to three-page essay every two weeks. If that is difficult for you, consider one or more of the following approaches.

Get Help.

As soon as your first paper is returned, see if you understand the teacher's comments and if you can use them when you are working on your next paper. **If at all doubtful, ask for a short conference.** Overcome your fear of a high profile. Let the teacher know you and know you are working. You will have a much better chance psychologically of tipping the grade in your favor. No teacher wants to give a D or F to someone he has helped all semester. If English is not your favorite subject, a C grade might be good enough for your purposes.

Have a good writer do a paper or two with you. Don't have this person write it, but talk out your topic together and then actually write it jointly. During the process observe how your friend thinks out a paper, what is considered and dropped, what is added—and why. Try to get the feel of the approach and imitate it on your own. Let your friend help you rewrite it. Like any other skill, composing is a knack. After three or four tries, you should begin to catch on.

Imitate a Model.

Most explanations are too abstract for a new writer to use effectively. So instead of feeling lost, carefully examine any example or sample the teacher uses. Work backwards from the example to the explanation, or just work with the example itself. Keep it in front of you when doing your own paper and try for a similar pattern and flow.

● **Pick as a model a magazine or newspaper article the length of the paper you want to write.** Pick a style fairly close to what you think your own would be.

● **Choose your own topic.** Always choose something you know inside out, upside down and backwards, if at all possible.

● **Then, using the model as your plan, compose a first paragraph imitating the model, sentence by sentence, varying the flow and rhythm, the sentence length and structure, in a similar way.** Put your main sentence in roughly the same location and have the same amount of supporting commentary.

● **Go on in this manner until your paper is completed.**

If you do this a few times, you will develop a framework for your own essays of this size.

Talk It Out.

● **If you have trouble getting words on paper, tell your essay to someone, letting them ask questions as you go, and record your conversation on tape.** Then just copy that onto paper, and you have your rough draft. That will give you a natural progression of thought and will probably have just enough detail to make it interesting and convincing. At any rate, you will have something you can tinker with.

Get a First Draft.

Don't worry about "composing." That usually results in clumsy, artificial wording, not anything like you.

● **First play with your topic, jotting down ideas and details. Put them in clusters as they occur to you.** Abbreviate. You should end up with three or four clusters. You may want to shift emphasis and move details around or drop or add some.

● **Next, write your first draft without stopping and without looking at your notes.** Don't worry about punctuation or wording. You can do that later. Write as though you were telling your idea to a younger brother or sister in, say, the eighth grade. You will know when they wouldn't understand, when they would need more explanation or detail, and when your idea is likely to be clear enough. The purpose of this approach is to get a clear and direct first draft with a good, rhythmic flow.

- **Now check your clusters and see if you left out anything really important.** Add those details where they fit smoothly.

- **Next read your first draft out loud and see how it sounds.** It should sound the way you normally talk. Get rid of any accidental confusion or expressions that don't sound like you. This will make you a good working draft, ready for editing and final polishing.

- **You will have to go through and proofread your paper at least four times. And you will have to make at least two drafts.** Make sure the copy you turn in is written or typed neatly. Sorry, there is no way to escape this. Subconsciously, teachers are deeply affected by insignificant errors and sloppiness. Anything you can do to make it look nice is worth the effort. Keep in mind that research shows there can be a letter-grade difference between a sloppy and neat version of the same paper.

EDITING AND POLISHING

If you were going to make a speech, your second draft might make a pretty good speech even without proofreading. Your usage would probably be acceptable to your audience, and they wouldn't see your spelling and punctuation. But if the paper is to be read instead of heard, then you will have to develop gradually some editing and polishing habits. **Once you are satisfied with the sound of your paper, proofread and polish until it is as error-free as you can make it.** These technical matters may not be an important part of your paper, but they are easy to look at and grade.

Usage

College teachers use a dialect somewhat different from students. Sometimes the gap is huge. They will expect you to use their dialect in your papers. What is perfectly okay among your acquaintances or on TV may not do. The solution is to learn their language. **One approach is to use a college English handbook. (More on that below.) Another is to become a keen observer of what most of us would consider unimportant differences in the way teachers and textbooks word their ideas.** Most English teachers don't expect you to use their vocabulary, but they will try to get you to follow their manner of speaking. Gradually, as you notice textbook usage and listen to teachers, you should be able to parody their dialect at will.

When you proofread, go through your paper and make your usage agree with your teacher's. Force yourself to check each sentence carefully, even if you have to lay a ruler under each line. If you have the least doubt, check it out. Ask a friend who is a good proofreader, or ask some other teacher. Get familiar with your English handbook.

Use a College English Handbook.

● **Buy yourself a college English handbook.** Keep it in your permanent library. Pick out one you like in your bookstore or ask a teacher whose judgment you value to suggest one. Leaf through the book frequently until you are sure you know what it contains and how to find it in a hurry. Many usages you may want to check will be alphabetized.

● **To use the handbook, find the item you have doubts about and imitate one of the examples.** Put a check in the margin each time you refer to that item. You will probably end up with not more than three checks.

Spelling

Take nothing for granted. **If you have the slightest doubt**

about a spelling, look it up. Get a small three-by-five dictionary. You will want it small enough for quick reference. Each
time you use it, put a check in the margin next to the word.
You can take spelling courses and learn rules, but this method
is all you really need. Good spelling comes from careful proofreading and close attention to the characteristics of each word.

When you find the word, take a good look at it syllable by
syllable. Is there a way to remember the spelling, any memory
device you can use? Write it out slowly and carefully, noticing
silent letters, double consonants, and so forth. See if you are
pronouncing it properly (*perform*, not *preform*; *tragedy*, not
tradegy). Is there a problem with the vowel or a consonant? Do
you confuse words that sound a bit alike (*affect* or *effect*)? Look
carefully at the difference; examine the examples. Separate
affixes and roots to see how they are formed. That will help
you to keep from using too few or too many letters (*mis spell*,
public ly). When you add a suffix, check to see if the final consonant of the root must be doubled or not (*plane*, *planing*; *plan*,
planning).

**It boils down to seeing, hearing, and writing the word
carefully and accurately.**

Don't expect miracles. At first you will have to use your
dictionary heavily, but if you do pay attention you will gradually form a habit of spelling most words you use correctly. Maintain a healthy distrust. To double check, have someone else
proofread after you finish.

Punctuation

● **Use your college English handbook.** Your questions will
mostly be about commas. Browse through the *comma* entry in
your handbook, paying close attention to the examples. When
you have a doubt, find an example just like your own sentence
and imitate that. You will have to look carefully. Sometimes
even the space between dots matters. Follow this same plan for
quotation marks, dashes, and parentheses.

Until you get used to the rules of punctuation, you can avoid difficult problems by rearranging your sentences or by making them into two or three shorter ones. Use as little internal punctuation as possible. When your sentence could be misread otherwise, insert the comma. A good test is to read it out loud.

Meanwhile, start observing punctuation in material you read. Many writers have never formally studied punctuation. They learn through observation.

Style

SOME WAYS TO IMPROVE STYLE

Rephrase all or part of a sentence.

Rearrange a sentence, putting a phrase or clause at the beginning or in the middle, instead of the end.

Combine two or more sentences, eliminating unnecessary repetition, using the same subject for a series of verbs, and so on.

Try breaking a cumbersome sentence into smaller ones.

Substitute other words when you find you have used the same expression over and over. Use a synonym every chance you get.

Get a college-sized dictionary (seven by ten or so) for your permanent library. Also, for synonyms, get a paperback thesaurus.

Paragraph frequently. It makes your paper seem organized.

If you can, let your paper cool for a day or so and then read it through again. You may find phrasing that doesn't sound good to you now. The more junk you can cut out,the better your paper will read.

SUMMARY

Get a first draft any way you can: using a model, talking into a tape, working with someone else, whatever. Read it out loud for sound and sense. Then proofread at least four times for usage, spelling, punctuation, and style. Let it sit overnight and read it again.

Keep the following books in your permanent library and have them close by when you write:

> Small spelling dictionary
> College English handbook
> Collegiate dictionary
> Thesaurus

In the meantime observe mechanics and style in materials you read. Imitate models you like, selecting those similar to your own way of talking.

Save every paper you write. You never know when one could be rewritten, expanded, or polished for another assignment.

BIBLIOGRAPHY

Bloom, Benjamin S. "Learning for Mastery," UCLA-CSEJP, *Evaluation Comment*, 1, number 2, 1968.

Carroll, John B. "A Model of School Learning," *Teachers College Record*, 64. 1963.

Carroll, John B. "Problems of Measurement Related to the Concept of Learning for Mastery," *Educational Horizons*, 48, number 3. 1970.

Cross, K. Patricia. *Beyond the Open Door*. Jossey-Bass. 1971.

Doerter, James. Unpublished research report. Southern Oregon College, Ashland, Oregon.

Glaser, Robert. "Ten Untenable Assumptions of College Instruction ," *Educational Record*. Spring 1968.

Jennings, Wayne, and Joe Nathan. "Startling/Disturbing Research on School Program Effectiveness," *Phi Delta Kappan*. March 1977.

Perry, William G. *Forms of Intellectual and Ethical Development in the College Years*. New York: Holt, Rinehart, and Winston, 1968.

Ruth, Leo. "Standardized Testing: How to Read the Results," SLATE Steering Committee Newsletter, NCTE/SLATE. Urbana, Illinois.

Staubach, Karl. "On Testing," Unpublished paper. Diablo Valley College, Pleasant Hill, California.

Whimbey, Arthur. "You Can Learn to Raise Your IQ Score," *Psychology Today*. January 1976.

INDEX

Time Use Chart

	MONDAY	TUESDAY	WEDNESDAY
8:00			
9:00			
10:00			
11:00			
12:00			
1:00			
2:00			
3:00			
4:00			
5:00			
6:00			
7:00			
8:00			
9:00			
10:00			

Include book title or subject, number of pages read, amount of time, and where you studied. Abbreviate.			
THURSDAY	FRIDAY	SATURDAY	SUNDAY

Time Use Chart

	MONDAY	TUESDAY	WEDNESDAY
8:00			
9:00			
10:00			
11:00			
12:00			
1:00			
2:00			
3:00			
4:00			
5:00			
6:00			
7:00			
8:00			
9:00			
10:00			

Include book title or subject, number of pages read, amount of time, and where you studied. Abbreviate.

THURSDAY	FRIDAY	SATURDAY	SUNDAY

Time Use Chart

	MONDAY	TUESDAY	WEDNESDAY
8:00			
9:00			
10:00			
11:00			
12:00			
1:00			
2:00			
3:00			
4:00			
5:00			
6:00			
7:00			
8:00			
9:00			
10:00			

Include book title or subject, number of pages read, amount of time, and where you studied. Abbreviate.

THURSDAY	FRIDAY	SATURDAY	SUNDAY

Time Use Chart

	MONDAY	TUESDAY	WEDNESDAY
8:00			
9:00			
10:00			
11:00			
12:00			
1:00			
2:00			
3:00			
4:00			
5:00			
6:00			
7:00			
8:00			
9:00			
10:00			

Include book title or subject, number of pages read, amount of time, and where you studied. Abbreviate.			
THURSDAY	FRIDAY	SATURDAY	SUNDAY

Time Use Chart

	MONDAY	TUESDAY	WEDNESDAY
8:00			
9:00			
10:00			
11:00			
12:00			
1:00			
2:00			
3:00			
4:00			
5:00			
6:00			
7:00			
8:00			
9:00			
10:00			

Include book title or subject, number of pages read, amount of time, and where you studied. Abbreviate.			
THURSDAY	FRIDAY	SATURDAY	SUNDAY

Clark McKowen teaches English at Diablo Valley College in Pleasant Hill, California. He is author of *Image: Reflections on Language* and co-author of *Montage: Investigations in Language*, freshman English texts published by Macmillan. He is co-author of *It's Only a Movie*, a film-appreciation book published by Prentice-Hall.

Get Your A Out of College reflects over twenty-two years of high school and college teaching and service as department and division chairman at both levels. The author has published articles on the teaching of English and on education and has conducted seminars on the educational process at various colleges throughout the United States.

Mr. McKowen is a graduate of Indiana State University in Indiana, Pennsylvania, and of Bucknell University in Lewisburg, Pennsylvania.